HIGH PRAISE FOR ONE OF THE YEAR'S MOST IMPRESSIVE BOOKS

"A clear and compelling account of the tangled series of world events which led predictably from the First to the Second World war.... The story is fascinating, told with verve.... It contains not only a lucid summary of this confusing era but also analytic digressions which probe the missions and motives of various national groups.... Goldston places people in events in perspective and demonstrates a thorough understanding of the time."
—*The Horn Book Magazine*

"Carefully interrelates international events, shifting power bases, and intrigues to portray the climate of the years between the two world wars... a colorful, smoothly written, detailed treatment... grist for history enthusiasts... incisive and interesting."
—*Booklist*

Also by Robert Goldston:

THE GREAT DEPRESSION

THE LIFE AND DEATH OF NAZI GERMANY

NEXT YEAR IN JERUSALEM

THE RUSSIAN REVOLUTION

The Road Between the Wars:

1918-1941

by ROBERT GOLDSTON

FAWCETT CREST • NEW YORK

THE ROAD BETWEEN THE WARS: 1918–1941

THIS BOOK CONTAINS THE COMPLETE TEXT OF THE
ORIGINAL HARDCOVER EDITION.

Published by Fawcett Crest Books, a unit of CBS Publica-
tions, the Consumer Publishing Division of CBS Inc., by arrangement with The Dial Press

ISBN: 0-449-24294-3

The author wishes to express his gratitude to Random House,
Inc., for permission to quote from "New Year Letter" by W.H.
Auden, from *Collected Poems of W.H. Auden*, edited by Ed-
ward Mendelson, © 1945 by Random House, Inc.

Printed in the United States of America

First Fawcett Crest printing: May 1980

10 9 8 7 6 5 4 3 2 1

For Claire Marguerite Hewitt,
who celebrates her own Armistice Day

CONTENTS

The Road Between the Wars:

1918-1941

PROLOGUE

All Quiet on the Western Front...

On the cold, gray, wet morning of November 8, 1918, Staff Sergeant James Conroy, Acting Platoon Leader in an American infantry company, lay on his belly in the underbrush of a small woods north of the Argonne Forest in France. Up ahead, hidden somewhere amid the dark shadows of the trees, German machine guns chattered. Each time they spoke, the air above Sergeant Conroy's head was filled with the angry whisper of bullets. Conroy pressed himself into the icy mud and cursed silently.

Only an hour earlier Sergeant Conroy's company, his battalion, his entire division, had clambered from their trenches with fixed bayonets. They had gone "over the top" willingly, even eagerly—for this would be the last big push of the war. And there would be no opposition. Battalion Headquarters had passed down the word—the Germans were pulling out, Fritz was on the run, the war was over, this advance would be a picnic. Sixty minutes later, having advanced exactly four hundred yards, Sergeant Conroy's platoon was badly hurt. The bodies of the dead and wounded lay scattered in the woods, hidden among the piles of dank, decaying leaves. The wounded groaned, called for help, sometimes shrieked—but no stretcher-bearers came. Like everyone else, the medics were pinned down by those angry whispers, punctuated now and then by the deafening roar of German artillery and the quiet *pop* of German gas shells which suffused the woods with a soft, white haze of deadly phosgene. Sergeant Conroy wondered bitterly just where in this leafy hell Battalion Headquarters was holding its picnic.

Of course he'd been tricked again. But that was normal. Sergeant Conroy felt he'd been tricked ever since he'd enlisted a year and a half earlier back in Chicago. He'd been tricked into imagining that war could be glamorous—tricked by the blaring bands, the flag-waving girls, the smart uniforms, the patriotic orators, the newspapers. For his own stupidity he really had no one to blame but himself. It was the other lies he'd believed, the big lies told by the big politicians, that deeply angered him. "They" had said he was going forth to rescue America's gallant allies, the British and French. But the English Tommies and French poilus he'd met were totally disillusioned, cynical, even mutinous after four years of war. His gallant allies didn't want to be rescued if that meant prolonging the agony. "They" had said he was embarked upon a crusade to "save Western civilization." But as far as Sergeant Conroy could see he was engaged in blowing up as much of that civilization as possible. "They" had said he would be fighting a cruel, barbarous, fiendishly evil enemy whose bloody conduct could be likened only to that of the Huns of old. But the miserable, war-weary, frightened German prisoners of war he'd seen stumbling along the roads behind the lines looked remarkably human, remarkably like himself and everyone else. And finally, "They" had said he would be battling "to make the world safe for democracy." On that promise Sergeant Conroy was willing to suspend judgment. No doubt the Germans did live under an autocratic tyranny, and maybe they really were intent on establishing their dictatorship over all of Europe or all the world. If they were defeated perhaps liberty and freedom and democracy, the big words Sergeant Conroy and his men still believed in, would triumph everywhere. Then there would be peace—everlasting peace, since no free men anywhere would ever willingly go to war again. Not after this. So maybe—just maybe—"They" had been telling the truth when they proclaimed this to be a "war to end all wars."

Meanwhile, the "defeated" Germans up ahead obstinately refused to realize they were beaten. They continued to fill the moist dawn air with death—perhaps they would counterattack. As he hugged the wet earth beneath him, Sergeant Conroy knew very well that he was not fighting for ideals, no matter how lofty, nor for words, no matter how big—he was simply fighting for his life.

On that same morning of November 8, far from the Argonne front, in another forest called Compiègne near the tiny French hamlet of Rothondes, Marshal Ferdinand Foch, Commander in Chief of all the Allied Armies, waited impatiently in a railroad car drawn up on a siding. The Marshal, a short, toughly built, white-mustached man in his sixties, whose gamecock stance always gave the impression that he was about to leap into action, had not slept all night. Now it was dawn and the visitors he awaited were twelve hours late. Twelve hours! While every minute of every day and every night a man was killed somewhere along the two hundred miles of battlefront. Those twelve hours had caused needless death. Needless because Marshal Foch was awaiting the arrival of a German delegation coming, they said, to seek an immediate armistice. An armistice would not stop the war (only peace treaties could do that), but it would stop the killing.

The immense, the unimaginable killing. Marshal Foch had no exact figures on casualties. He knew his own French armies had suffered nearly one and a half million deaths; that his British allies had lost nearly a million dead; that his Italian allies had lost more than half a million; that the late-arriving Americans had already suffered some three hundred thousand casualties. He estimated that the Germans had lost nearly two million dead, and their Austrian and Turkish allies another million and a half between them. And what of the Russians? Who could even guess at their losses? At least two million dead. And how many civilians had perished? All of Europe had become a charnel house. And with every further minute of delay the endless killing went on. Not only the killing—but also the destruction that was turning a continent into a wasteland.

It must end. But it must end in victory—on Allied terms. The Germans had started the war. They had invaded and occupied all of Belgium and Luxembourg, most of north-eastern France, much of Russia. They must evacuate every inch of this conquered territory. And they must return to France the provinces of Alsace and Lorraine which they had seized in 1870. To be certain that they could never again plunge Europe into catastrophe, the Germans must disband their armies and fleets, totally disarm, and pay a crushing war-reparations bill. To ensure their compliance Allied armies would occupy all of Germany west of the river Rhine. It was important that the Germans *know* they had been beaten.

Marshal Foch considered these terms moderate. Not so moderate perhaps as those proposed by the English commander, Field Marshal Sir Douglas Haig, who was willing to settle simply for German evacuation of the occupied territories and Alsace-Lorraine. But the English had not suffered a German occupation. Their towns and cities and fields had not been destroyed by German guns. Not sharing a common border with Germany, they had not, like France, been invaded by Germans twice within fifty years. Just as the English Channel protected Britain, so the wide sweep of the Rhine must protect France. Certainly, Foch thought, his terms were milder than those the triumphant Germans had forced on defeated Russia a few months earlier when they had signed a treaty at Brest Litovsk; and they were even milder than those proposed by the American commander, General John J. Pershing. "Black Jack" (as he was called for reasons incomprehensible to Marshal Foch) had wanted to march straight on to Berlin and dictate a peace of "unconditional surrender" in the German capital. But Pershing's forces were still relatively fresh. Their casualties had not yet mounted into the millions. The American "doughboys" (another mysterious Yankee term) still fought willingly, even eagerly. But the British and French were exhausted. The world did not yet know—Marshal Foch had seen to that—that many French regiments were in a state of mutiny. Some had murdered their officers, thrown down their guns, and refused to fight on. The Marshal had ordered executions. Order had been restored. But the French Army had lost its morale—it would not march on to Berlin.

An armistice was therefore necessary. When Colonel Edward House, the personal emissary of American President Woodrow Wilson, had asked the Marshal about this, Foch had replied, "I am not waging war for the sake of waging war. If I obtain through the armistice the terms we wish to impose upon Germany, I am satisfied. Once this object is attained nobody has the right to shed one more drop of blood."

Now it was seven in the morning, and where were the Germans? Just then Marshal Foch heard, above the incessant rain, the sigh of air brakes. The train bearing the German delegation had at last arrived. Foch's Chief of Staff, General Maxime Weygand, opened the compartment door.

"Here they are, *mon Maréchal*."

Foch peered out the window. Over the morass of yellow mud between Foch's train and the newly arrived German train, French soldiers were laying a walk of boards tied together with rope. Four men emerged from the German train.

"So this," muttered Foch, "is the German Empire. We will meet at nine."

In his "office car," furnished with a large central table surrounded by a dozen leather-upholstered chairs, Foch and a small group of French, British, and American officers gathered. Precisely at nine A.M. the Germans—Matthias Erzberger and Count Alfred Obendorff representing the new German government, General Detlef von Winterfeldt representing the German Army, and Captain Hans Vanselow representing the German Navy—entered the car and took seats pointed out to them.

"What is the purpose of your visit?" Foch demanded.

Erzberger looked startled. "Why— Of course, we have come to ask for—to receive the proposals of the Allied Powers—looking to an armistice..."

"I have no proposals to make," Foch replied.

"What do you want us to say?" Count Obendorff asked. "I do not stand on form. I am ready to say this German delegation asks the conditions of the armistice."

"I have no conditions to offer," Foch replied.

"But," said Erzberger, "President Wilson authorized Marshal Foch to make known to us the armistice conditions."

"Only if," Foch said, "the German delegation asks for an armistice. Do you ask for an armistice? If you do, I can inform you of the conditions on which it may be obtained."

"We ask for an armistice," Erzberger mumbled.

"We ask for an armistice," Obendorff echoed.

Foch began to read from a sheaf of papers. "The immediate evacuation of all lands unlawfully invaded, Belgium, France, Alsace-Lorraine, and Luxembourg . . . Surrender by the enemy of 5,000 cannon, 30,000 machine guns...Evacuation by the German Army of all territory on the left bank of the Rhine; occupation by the Allies of Mainz, Koblenz, Cologne, and Strasbourg...Delivery of 5,000 locomotives and 150,000 railway cars...Delivery of 150 submarines, withdrawal of the surface fleet to Baltic ports, occupation by the Allied fleets of Cuxhaven and Helgoland . . . Maintenance of the blockade during the period fixed for the fulfillment of the above conditions."

Erzberger was almost in tears at the end of this reading. He asked for a suspension of military operations during negotiations. He admitted that the German Army was demoralized, disorganized, and undisciplined. He warned that if Allied attacks continued, Communist rebellion might sweep Germany. Bolshevism might then spread to France and England.

Foch waved impatiently. "Western Europe will find means of defending itself against the danger," he said drily.

The German delegates asked for a delay. Foch refused. The Armistice must be signed on November 11, at eleven A.M.—not one minute later. Until it was signed, the Allied armies would press relentlessly forward.

The German delegates retired to their own train. From there they sent telegrams and a special courier to German Supreme Headquarters at Spa. Then they waited. On November 9, Marshal Foch ordered that the Allied offensive be intensified. *"Tout le monde à la bataille!"*—"Everyone into battle!"—was always his motto. On the evening of November 10, the Marshal reminded the German delegates that only twelve hours remained for their reply. After that time Allied terms would change—for the worse. A few hours later, near midnight on November 10, came a long telegram from the German Supreme Commander, Field Marshal Paul von Hindenburg. It was full of protest, excuses, and self-pity—but it accepted the Allied terms.

At five in the morning on November 11, the German delegation, once again assembled in Foch's railway car, signed the Armistice arrangements. Firing was to cease on all fronts at eleven A.M. that same morning.

Marshal Foch at once sat down to compose a General Order to all the Allied forces. "You have won," he wrote, "the greatest battle in history, and rescued the most sacred of all causes, the Liberty of the World."

In Paris that morning, hundreds of thousands of people congregated along the grand boulevards, at the Place de la Concord, the Place de la Bastille, the Rond Point, the Arc de Triomphe. They drank thousands of liters of good French wine and champagne; they danced in the streets, hugged each other, shouted for joy, wept, cheered, and sang. They sang the wartime favorites, "La Madelon," "Sambre et Meuse," the lionhearted "Sidi Brahmin" and, passionately, "La Marseillaise." For this was *le jour de gloire*—the day of glory. Anyone in uniform—especially anyone in an American uniform—was engulfed with tears, kisses, good wishes. Thousands cheered as President Raymond Poincaré and Premier Georges Clemenceau—the Tiger of France—motored down the Champs-Élysées on their way to the *Chambre des Députés,* the French parliament.

But there was a somber undercurrent to this vast celebration. Too many in the crowds mourned loved ones; too many knew that France had been bled white during the struggle. Her young manhood had perished in a thousand battles—at the river Marne, along the rivers Aisne and Meuse, at Charleroi, Épinal, Toul, and the endless hell of Verdun. It must never happen again. France could not survive another German invasion. Never again must the Teutonic hordes come pouring down the pleasant lanes and tree-lined roads of France. Poincaré and Clemenceau would see to that. But if national security came first, there were many in the joyous crowds who hoped for something more.

The American President, Woodrow Wilson, had spoken of a world forever free of war, of a new League of Nations which would forever preserve peace. Wilson, with all the vigor of a youthful, idealistic, and powerful nation behind him, had brought new hope to war-weary French hearts. It was that hope, as much as the victory, that Parisians celebrated on November 11.

In London, as the news of the Armistice came over the wireless, more than two million people thronged the streets. They jammed Piccadilly Circus and Trafalgar Square and Hyde Park and the Mall leading to Buckingham Palace. For once dropping traditional British reserve, total strangers embraced and danced together in the streets. Pubs served free beer and ale. Thousands of hoarse voices were raised to sing "Tipperary," "There's a Long, Long Trail A-Winding," "Pack up Your Troubles," and, with deep emotion, "God Save the King." And they cheered. They cheered the appearance of King George V and the royal family on the balcony of "Buck House," they cheered the limousines that carried Prime Minister David Lloyd George and Munitions Minister (formerly First Lord of the Admiralty) Winston Churchill to Parliament. Like Parisians a few hundred kilometers away beyond the English Channel, they were cheering their victory and their hopes and, please God, never again.

For nearly a million Englishmen would never return from the battlefields of France. They had fallen at Mons and Ypres and along the river Somme, and their bodies rested in Flanders' fields. Thousands more were buried in far-off Turkish Gallipoli and in Palestine, and very many were buried beneath the cold waters of the North Atlantic. To be sure, the Empire had emerged intact and triumphant; but the cost had been too great. It would not do to return to the prewar policies that had been unable to prevent war—a new world order would have to be built. Like the French, the English people placed their hope and faith in the words of Woodrow Wilson. They knew of his "Fourteen Points" which had been offered as the basis for peace. They knew that Wilson and America had no selfish motives. And they believed that Wilson saw farther into the future than their own leaders. With confidence in Wilson's vision of a world ordered by law and reason Londoners celebrated the advent of eternal peace on November 11.

In distant, snow-clad Moscow (which had replaced St. Petersburg as the capital of Russia after the Bolshevik seizure of power in October 1917) there was no outpouring of people into the streets, no general rejoicing at the news of the Armistice in the West. For Russia, under the guidance of her revolutionary leaders, Vladimir Lenin and Leon Trotsky, was already at peace with Germany, if not with herself. The victorious Germans had dictated their terms to Russia in the White Russian town of Brest Litovsk in March 1918. And despite all Trotsky's cunning at the conference table, those terms had been harsh. Russia lost Finland, Poland, the Baltic States, the Ukraine—34 percent of her population, 32 percent of her agricultural land, 54 percent of her industry, 89 percent of her coal mines. But then, Russia had been utterly defeated. And now the entire nation was wracked by civil war between the newly organized Bolshevik, or "Red," Army and various Tsarist "White" armies.

Nor were Russian towns occupied only by Germans. For the Allies, proclaiming that the triumphant Germans might seize various important munitions and supply dumps, had occupied Murmansk, Archangel, and even Vladivostok (more than three thousand miles from the nearest triumphant Germans). These occupation forces—British in Murmansk-Archangel, American and Japanese in Vladivostok—engaged in countless small battles against local Bolshevik militias. And, to cap matters, a Czech "army" of some thirty thousand men (former Tsarist prisoners of war set free by the Bolsheviks) were marching along the Trans-Siberian Railroad to the Far East, whence they expected to take ships for Europe and so return to their homeland the long way. These Czechs fought anyone, Red or White, who stood in their way. Russia was in utter chaos.

Yet Lenin and Trotsky entertained high hopes for the future. They confidently awaited the Communist revolutions which, according to their theory, would now sweep all of Western Europe. When the Red flag floated above Paris, London, and Berlin, then the detestable Peace of Brest Litovsk would simply be discarded. Russia would emerge whole and healed from her long agony.

Matters had not quite worked out that way. Before the Allied fighting men turned their weapons against their "oppressors" they used them to rout the Germans. And although Communist riots, mutinies, and uprisings were sweeping Germany, the Allied nations were emerging from the war in solid capitalistic power. French and British leaders had long since denounced the Bolshevik revolution (Winston Churchill regretted he could not "strangle it in the cradle")—but the American attitude was not yet certain. Woodrow Wilson had welcomed the overthrow of the Tsar—and, unlike the British and French, the Americans did not intrigue to overthrow the Bolshevik Government. If Wilson really meant what he said about the right of all peoples to choose their own form of government, about a peace without vengeance, and about his League of Nations, then there was still reason to hope. Of course, in the long run Communism and capitalism could never coexist peacefully on the same planet. But at least for now, if Wilson had his way, Russia would apparently be restored, welcomed back into the family of nations and left in peace to pursue her "new path into the future." So, although the people of Moscow, engulfed in their own tragedy, barely noticed the news of the Armistice, Lenin, Trotsky, and their fellow Bolshevik leaders warily welcomed it.

Berlin, on November 11, 1918, was a city under siege from within. No crowds of celebrating civilians poured out into the Wilhelmstrasse or Unter den Linden—for the streets of the city were not safe. Rightist gangs, Leftist gangs, and criminal gangs (who could tell the difference among them?) were waging a small but intense guerrilla war in the German capital. In Munich and other cities, it was rumored, the Red flag already floated above city halls. The fleet had mutinied in Kiel and Bolshevik agitators were now leading the sailors. The Kaiser had fled over the border into neutral Holland, the generals disclaimed all responsibility (they were still "unbeaten in the field," they claimed) and although there was now some sort of Social-Democratic government sitting in the Chancellory in Berlin, who knew how long it could last? After four years of British sea blockade the German people were nearly starving, and as everyone knew, the armies were disintegrating. Germany was sliding toward total ruin, total disorder—a condition most hateful to the German soul.

And yet they had come so close, so very close to winning. It was only the entry of the United States into the war which made German defeat certain. But now, paradoxically, it was America's presence in the ranks of her enemies that provided Germans with some shreds of hope for the future. When Woodrow Wilson had first offered his "Fourteen Points" as a possible basis for peace, Field Marshal von Hindenburg and Chief of Staff General Erich Ludendorff (after four years of war the virtual dictators of Germany) had dismissed them contemptuously. That had been early in 1918, when Ludendorff, employing German forces released from the now-quiet Russian front, had expected to crush the British and French before the Americans arrived in strength. Now, ten months later, with the British and French uncrushed and a million Americans hammering toward the Rhine, the German General Staff grasped at Wilson's proposals like drowning men clutching the sides of a lifeboat. The German delegation to Compiègne had gone armed with a copy of Wilson's declaration when they signed the Armistice.

As for the German people—mourning nearly two million dead, disillusioned and bitter against the men who had led them to disaster—they too clung to Wilson's ideas. There would be a peace without vengeance. Germany would, of course, have to give up her conquests—but since all peoples would enjoy the right of self-determination, German territory would not be seized. The German people would not be blamed for their leaders' mistakes. Now that they had established a democratic government (however shaky), Germans would be accepted into the new League of Nations on a basis of equality. Germany's legitimate rights would be respected, her peaceful aspirations encouraged. With the truth of total defeat and potential chaos staring them in the face, the German people might not cheer the Armistice—but by and large they greeted it with an almost audible sigh of relief.

*   *   *

On a grassy hilltop about twenty miles beyond the Argonne Forest, Sergeant Conroy and the remnants of his platoon waited for the war to end. Just three days before, they had been pinned down by German machine guns in a small woods where they had left sixteen dead comrades. But the machine gunning had ended—suddenly, mysteriously. A captain had come forward with orders to advance. They had done so—cautiously at first, then with increasing boldness. They had found those German machine guns—perfectly emplaced and completely abandoned. Slowly it began to dawn on them that the Germans were no longer even going to fight rearguard actions to cover their general retreat. Conroy and his men walked more confidently down the dusty roads. They passed German supply dumps, German artillery, German trenches, German barracks— all deserted. There was no more resistance. And their advance had brought them, finally, to this grassy knoll. They had been told there would be an armistice at eleven A.M. that day. Now, with only a few minutes to go before eleven, they had begun to realize that, incredibly, they were all going to survive this war. They would be going home.

They waited in silence—each man too full of thought to speak. But though they were quiet, the day was not. To the south could be heard the rattle of rifle fire and machine guns, to the north a tremendous thundering which had just started. Some maniac, Sergeant Conroy thought, getting off one last artillery barrage, one last salvo of death—completely unnecessary, vicious, murderous. The sergeant felt a wave of rage rise in him at all the senseless killing. . . .

And then the thunder died away and the distant machine guns were stilled. It was just eleven A.M., and what Sergeant Conroy would always remember about that moment was the sudden, deafening silence. For once, he reflected, the newspaper correspondents could truthfully report: All quiet on the Western front.

> *My message today was a message*
> *of death for our young men.*
>
> WOODROW WILSON

1

The Last Crusade

The world that gave birth to what would be called (until
1939) the Great War was a much more dramatic place
than it has been since. Most of it was still ruled by
kings, emperors, kaisers, and tsars. And even though
these glittering figures exercised, for the most part,
only nominal power, they and their royal families, ar-
istocracies, palaces, crowns, and pomp and circum-
stance held very real sway over people's imagination.
They provided a cherished link with the past, and were
living symbols of order, continuity, and predictability
in human affairs. So potent were these symbols that
even in those few countries (such as France and the

United States) which had dispensed with monarchy, people expressed a desire for it. In France they did so very consciously through the never-ending intrigues and machinations of Bonapartists, Orleanists, and Bourbons whose open or covert attacks upon the Third Republic kept French politics in a constant state of uproar. In the United States people satisfied their yearning for royalty through the wistful creation of play titles for countless members of clubs, lodges, orders, and fraternal organizations. Compared to royalty, the presidents, prime ministers, premiers, and chancellors—the men who held real power—seemed pale, drab figures.

Indeed, politicians were not even second in the social pecking order. That place was reserved for the rich. Not as yet vexed by heavy income and inheritance taxes, the wealthy everywhere—in England as in Germany, in Russia as in the United States—enjoyed a life of mansions, carriages, servants; of ease, opulence, and garish display beyond compare. Furthermore, they enjoyed this life in an all-but-unshakable sense of complete security and with few, if any, twinges of shame. Their wealth was, for the most part, derived from the financing, direction, and exploitation of an Industrial Revolution which had, within the space of a century, transformed life on earth and people's view of the cosmos. By extending Charles Darwin's recently established theory of evolution into the social sphere it was easy to demonstrate that those who, through harder work, greater ruthlessness, and deeper cunning, assured the economic survival of the species were themselves the fittest to survive. Besides, the well-being of the rich assured the prosperity of the growing middle classes and even the humble bread of the vast masses of the poor. For, as everyone knew, wealth trickled down from above. Any interference with the delicate machinery of capitalism, any restraint upon vigorously free enterprise, would not only be immoral, it would be unscientifically counterproductive. Everywhere in the world, either directly or indirectly, the rich controlled the governments; after all, those who created society's wealth should be the ones to lead it.

With that last view, socialists everywhere were in agreement. They did not, however, believe that society's wealth was created by the rich, but rather by the harshly exploited labor of the suffering poor, the working class. With a tradition of protest going back to the days of the French Revolution, socialist thinkers— Saint-Simon, Fourier, Owen, Marx, Engels—had developed a different view of industrial society. Capitalism—the private ownership of the means of production—was a harsh but probably necessary means of industrialization. It had been a step forward from the old mercantile-feudal order. But now, in the West at least, that step had been taken. And industrialization, far from creating its promised economic heaven, had created a veritable hell on earth for the great majority of people. This was because the fruits of industrial progress were hoarded by the greedy possessor classes. Capitalism, which had created the industrial world, had now become a tyranny and an obstacle to further progress. To be sure, Karl Marx had definitely demonstrated that this tyranny, in the long run, would be self-liquidating. As capitalist competition concentrated wealth in fewer and fewer hands, as capitalist governments, competing for raw materials and trade, were driven into mutually suicidal wars, as the insatiable desire for profits reduced the working classes everywhere to deeper and deeper misery, there would inevitably be an explosion. The desperate proletariat would rise to destroy its oppressors. Then socialism—the social or public ownership of the means of production—would create a classless society and usher in mankind's golden age.

Although this social apocalypse was "inevitable," it was the duty of socialists to hasten it along—by organizing workers into labor unions and political parties through which they might ameliorate their deplorable conditions, educate themselves in socialist doctrine, and gain a sense of class consciousness, of international proletarian solidarity. Various Socialist parties in Europe and America quarreled bitterly among themselves about what means they should use to achieve their goals, but they were in general agreement about their desired ends. Since 1889 Socialist parties had adhered to the Second International Workingmen's Association, and had sent representatives to annual meetings of the Second International in various European cities. There they argued among themselves and issued harmless proclamations. Harmless because in no country, despite their growing membership (Socialist parties claimed more than four million followers throughout the world in 1910), were Socialists in power—or even viewed as close to power. The bastions of capitalism, defended by law, usage, the police, and armies, remained secure. Of course Russian socialists, following tsarist Russia's defeat by Japan in 1905, had led a revolution; they had even exercised power briefly in Moscow and St. Petersburg. But the Tsar had soon found means to crush that revolt.

Although the ramparts of privilege were strong, they were not totally unassailable. This had been bloodily demonstrated by a scattered handful of anarchists. Despising the ploddingly pedestrian pace of socialist propaganda and education, driven by despair to reject any and all forms of social organization, anarchists demanded revolution now. And they sought to ignite it by "propaganda of the deed"—individual acts of terror which would cow the ruling classes and embolden the oppressed. To anarchist guns, knives, and explosives fell no less than six heads of state in the two decades before 1914. They included President Carnot of France, two Spanish premiers, Empress Elisabeth of Austria-Hungary, King Umberto of Italy, and President McKinley of the United States. These and other assassinations had ignited not revolution but worldwide revulsion, which workers shared equally with capitalists. Yet they were a symptom—a signal from the lower depths that social pressures were growing unbearable.

There were other signals—and governments responded to them in different ways. In England the ruling aristocracy and the rich were grudgingly making room for the working class in the seats of power. A Labor Party had been organized, and had even won a few seats in Parliament. In France, where the powerful trade unions were socialist-dominated, working-class leaders sat in the Chamber of Deputies and one or two even held Cabinet positions. In Germany, whose Social-Democratic Party was the world's largest and best organized, Socialists were the strongest group in the *Reichstag*—the Parliament. But since the Reichstag was utterly powerless in any event, they represented no real threat to the ruling autocracy. In the United States, which had never had a class-bound society, which enjoyed an ever-expanding economy and the vast labor-dumping ground of the West, socialism made little political headway. But various reformist movements, especially populism, steadily eroded economic inequality and social privilege. Trade unions were gathering strength, and explosive protest issues were dealt with one by one in typically American pragmatic fashion. Tsarist Russia, of course, remained an absolute tyranny supported by vast police terror. All in all, the world might be troubled by its masses—but not threatened by them.

Of course, when one spoke in these terms of "the world," before 1914, one meant only Europe and North America; nothing else really mattered. Africa, Asia, and South America were simply vast reservoirs of free raw materials and labor and captive markets for manufactured goods. Such places were inhabited by "lesser breeds without the law," by ignorant heathens who were there to be exploited, governed, enslaved, and otherwise blessed with Christian civilization. The white man had been selected by God for this divine task. Africa had been divided between France and England (with a small portion left over for Germany); India and fully one quarter of all the rest of the world formed that British Empire upon which the sun never set; South America remained the preserve of Yankee "dollar diplomacy"; and the Far East was rapidly being gobbled up. England, France, Germany, Russia, and Japan were quarreling over the dying carcass of the Chinese empire while the United States, exporting its native racism, had only recently subdued the Philippines after a bloody guerrilla war. It was the heyday of imperialism—Europeans and Americans manfully assumed the White Man's Burden, and most of them really believed it to be a work of Providential charity.

It was, in fact, this very ability to *believe* that most distinguished the prewar world from what came after. Though they might be divided politically and nationally, though they might place different interpretations upon words, most Westerners before 1914, rich or poor, capitalist, socialist, or monarchist, truly believed in God, Duty, Country, Honor, Gallantry, and Progress—especially Progress. They shared an unshakable confidence in the future of man. Having come so far in just a century of Industrial Revolution, people were optimistic about that future. The ancient enemies of mankind, disease and hunger, were being vanquished by education and scientific progress. Even the scourge of war would soon be lifted. Already two international conferences had been held at The Hague in Holland to discuss disarmament, international law, and the peaceful settlement of international disputes. True, little progress had been made—but these first trembling steps toward universal peace held great promise. Above all, man's fierce passions were being slowly but surely subdued by his "better nature," by his "unconquerable mind." The self-assurance engendered by these beliefs imparted a dignity to individual lives which has not been known since. For this was the world basking in the golden sunset of an era—a world upon which its survivors would always look back with nostalgic regret. There was no leader of the prewar world more self-assured than Woodrow Wilson, onetime President of Princeton University, later Governor of New Jersey and, from March 4, 1913, President of the United States. A lean, distinguished, stubborn-jawed gentleman whose frosty blue eyes peered haughtily at the world through pince-nez spectacles, Wilson was one of the very few examples in history of the intellectual as a successful politician. Actually his election in 1912 had been a fluke—brought about by a split in the majority Republican Party. That year a sizable bloc of Republicans led by former President Theodore Roosevelt, who felt that the incumbent President William Howard Taft had betrayed "progressive" principles, deserted the regular Taft ticket to follow Roosevelt's new Progressive ("Bull Moose") Party. As a result, with much less than a majority of the votes, Wilson became the second Democratic President since the Civil War.

Wilson was an unbending idealist—reserved in manner (no one was ever known to call him "Woody" or "W.W.") and utterly convinced of the rightness of his views. His campaign speeches calling for economic and social reform (he called his program "The New Freedom") rang with the eloquence of a Puritan preacher. He had inherited the leadership of the Democratic Party from the "radical" Populist William Jennings Bryan. And although he looked upon Bryan's simpleminded cure-all solutions with contempt, Wilson adopted much of the old Populist platform. The basic problem facing America after the turn of the century was that industry and finance—lumped together in the popular imagination as "big business" or "the trusts," unfettered by government regulation, and unrestrained by what were then weak and powerless trade unions—ran roughshod over American life. American industry had been, since the turn of the century, the world's largest—but boom and bust followed each other in painful twenty-five year cycles. Farmers were at the mercy of railroads and food packers and the banks, while industrial workers enjoyed no rights at all. Wages were abysmally low, hours painfully long, job security unknown, child labor and sweatshop conditions the norm. With their monopolistic stranglehold on the nation's economy, giant corporations (who "bought" entire state governments and hired armies of Pinkerton's detectives as thugs to enforce their will) were reducing farmers and workers to a kind of economic and social serfdom.

On this analysis both Roosevelt and Wilson were

agreed. But while Roosevelt felt that bigness and monopoly were the natural, efficient, logical outcome of industrialization, and required only government regulation, Wilson decried bigness as a curse in itself. If government attempted to regulate the monopolies it would itself merely become another soulless giant. Bigness, in industry or government, was to be avoided. The solution was to break up the huge industrial units and encourage competition among smaller enterprises—that was the true role of government.

Eventually, under wartime pressures, Wilson would come around to Roosevelt's viewpoint. But war was, of course, the furthest thing from the President's mind in 1914. Not that Wilson was shy about using American power on the international stage; when, in 1915–1916, the troubled pot of Mexican politics boiled over into revolution, he did not hesitate to send "Black Jack" Pershing and the Cavalry over the border on a "Punitive Expedition," nor did he balk at ordering a U.S. fleet to bombard Vera Cruz and land U.S. Marines to "protect American interests." But the idea of a major war was to him anathema; it was barbaric, loathsome—and would interrupt his cherished program of domestic reform.

Indeed, war was very far from the minds of the American people in 1914. The United States had not engaged in any major conflict since 1865—the brief imperialistic savagery with which Americans had fallen upon the hapless Spaniards in 1898 hardly counted, any more than the campaigns against the Plains Indians out West (the last one had been concluded in 1910). Americans were absorbed in their own affairs. They argued about the trusts, about the new income tax, about prohibition and women's suffrage, about the rights of trade unions, about the tides of immigration which had brought more than six million Europeans to their shores since 1890, about the spreading radicalism of the Industrial Workers of the World ("Wobblies") who preached the overthrow of capitalism through "one big strike." And they busied themselves with the development of such newfangled gadgets as automobiles, electric lights, telephones, and motion pictures. Despite the ancient grievances of the poor, the ancient arrogance of the rich, despite the fact that the Census Bureau had announced there no longer existed a Western frontier, Americans were even more optimistic about the future than Europeans. After all, Europe was still a continent of kings and aristocrats and classes and militarism—the entire hateful apparatus of the Old World. But America was the land of opportunity, the peace-loving great republic, still Lincoln's "last, best hope of earth." When the bands played "The Star-Spangled Banner" people stood at attention with unashamed, simple, fervent patriotism. It was not complicated to be an American in the years before 1914.

Germany's "Iron Chancellor," Otto von Bismarck, had once predicted that the next great European war would be touched off by "some damned foolish thing in the Balkans." As usual, he was right. The damned foolish thing turned out to be the assassination, by Serbian superpatriots, of the Archduke Franz Ferdinand and his wife in Sarajevo on June 28, 1914. The Archduke was heir apparent to the throne of the Austro-Hungarian Empire, and in his murder Austrian Emperor Franz Josef saw the opportunity to annex Serbia to his ramshackle domains.

Those domains, which included Austrians, Hungarians, Slavs, Czechs, Serbs, Croats, Slovenes, and a dozen other submerged nationalities, were deeply trou-

Europe in 1914

bled in the decade before 1914. Disgusted by the decadent Hapsburg tyranny that weighed upon them from Vienna, the peoples of the Austro-Hungarian Empire yearned for national independence. Their yearnings were encouraged by Balkan nations such as Bulgaria, Rumania, and Serbia (which had only recently won independence from the Turkish Empire). The Hapsburg solution was simple: Conquer these small Balkan nations ard they would no longer trouble the imperial peace. With this in mind, the Empire had absorbed the two formerly Turkish provinces of Bosnia and Herzegovina in 1912; now it would be the turn of the subversive Serbs. Accordingly, the Austro-Hungarian government issued a severe, all-but-unacceptable ultimatum to the Serbs and, even though Serbia unexpectedly agreed to abide by almost all its terms, began to bombard the Serbian capital, Belgrade, on July 29, 1914.

All of which was watched with mounting apprehension and anger by imperial Russia. The tsarist government, traditional foe of Austro-Hungarian expansion into the Balkans and self-proclaimed "protector" of all Slavs everywhere, felt it could not stand idly by while the Hapsburgs gobbled up yet another small Slav nation. Having suffered a humiliating defeat at the hands of the Japanese in the Far East just nine years earlier, and a subsequent revolution at home, the empty-headed Tsar Nicholas II and his equally empty-headed ministers feared that the Romanov dynasty might not survive yet another blow to its prestige. So Russia mobilized threateningly along her Austro-Hungarian borders.

This eventuality had not, of course, been hidden from the Austrians. But they counted upon aid from a powerful ally—Germany. Indeed, before taking action against the Serbs, the Austrians had checked with the Germans and been advised to proceed. As German Kaiser Wilhelm II had once declared in one of his less modest pronouncements, he stood beside his Hapsburg ally "in shining armor."

Now, with the Russians threatening Austria-Hungary, the German government dispatched a note to St. Petersburg demanding that Russia demobilize within twenty-four hours "and make us a distinct declaration to that effect." When the Russians ignored this demand, Germany declared war.

As the Germans well knew, Russia also had an ally— France. In fact it was against France first, and only later Russia, that the German General Staff had long planned to strike. At the same time as they sent their note to St. Petersburg, the Kaiser's ministers also sent an ultimatum to Paris demanding to know whether or not France would fight alongside Russia. If not, then she must hand over to German "safekeeping" her border fortresses of Toul, Épinal, and Verdun as "guarantees" of her neutrality. When French Premier René Viviani coldly informed the German ambassador that France "would consult her own interests," Germany declared war upon her too. Whether this would bring into the war France's partner, England, was for the moment a matter of no concern to the German High Command. And so the entire rickety structure of European peace came crashing down because of the "frivolous bellicosity" of two senile empires—neither of which would survive the war.

Germany, whose generals declared themselves to be "superready" for the struggle, went to war with a feeling not merely of righteousness, but of exhilaration. The sword, they felt, had been forced into their hand— by Russia's clumsy ambitions in the Balkans, by

France's insatiable desire for revenge for the defeat inflicted upon her in 1870, by England's obvious determination to stamp out German competition. Ever since 1870 Germany had been struggling to achieve her rightful "place in the sun," had been fighting against "encirclement," had been striving to assume what she considered her true status among nations—the status of the greatest.

Germans entered the twentieth century with a sense of aggrieved repression. France had her art, her culture, her traditions of the Great Revolution; England had her huge Empire. But what did Germany have? Germans, who had lost their own liberal revolution of 1848, who came late to nationhood, whose political life was an empty mockery, who were ruled by an autocratic caste of Prussian *Junkers*, landed aristocrats, wealthy industrialists, militaristic field marshals, and a kaiser who sincerely believed in his divine right as the all-highest, impatiently awaited their moment in history. They listened eagerly to philosophers such as Johann Fichte and Georg Hegel, who told them they'd been chosen by Providence to rule the universe; to Friedrich Nietzsche, who urged them to be supermen; to Heinrich von Treitschke, who taught them they owed absolute obedience to the State. Germans worked diligently, and were conscious of their power. Was not German industry the mightiest in Europe? Was not the German educational system the envy of the world? Was not German *Kultur*—especially in music and science—the most vital? Was not the German Army the greatest military machine ever devised? Was not German life a model to which all peoples aspired? Why then did other nations obstinately refuse to accept German supremacy? Why did England, France, and Russia incessantly scheme and plot (there could be no doubt of it) to thwart every honest German ambition? If Germany's claim to preeminence could not be achieved by peaceful means, then it must be won by the sword.

Bismarck, the architect of the German Empire, had been a realist. He had opposed the seizure of Alsace-Lorraine from France after the victory of 1870—precisely because that would stimulate French hatred; he had been careful to maintain a "reinsurance treaty" with Russia (so that if Germany and France ever did come to blows again, Germany would not have to fight a two-front war); he had urged the Kaiser to be content with the world's most powerful army and not to build a huge navy which could only threaten and, eventually, alienate Great Britain. Bismarck understood very clearly that in order to preserve the power of the anachronistic Junker class, and also that of the royal Hohenzollern family in a modern, industrialized state, it was essential not to upset the international status quo. For that could bring pressures to bear upon the German autocracy which it might not survive.

By 1890, however, Germans were thoroughly dissatisfied with the status quo. That year the young Kaiser Wilhelm II dismissed Bismarck and, guided by woolly-headed ministers, embarked upon a more adventurous policy. The German government dreamed of a *Drang nach Osten,* Drive to the East, that would annex huge areas of Russia for "living space"; it dreamed of crushing France once and for all; it dreamed of taking over large parts of the British Empire. Within ten years they managed to make every mistake against which Bismarck had warned. German dreams, ambitions, supernationalism, careened like a battleship out of control through the troubled waters of European diplomacy for two decades.

In the end, German fears were self-fulfilling. Threatened by strident German ambitions, France, Russia, and England did indeed attempt to encircle Germany in an effort to contain her. When, in July 1914, Kaiser Wilhelm offhandedly assured Emperor Franz Josef that Austria-Hungary could count on German support against Russia, he did not really believe that this latest crisis would lead to war. A few weeks later, on the lip of catastrophe, the German government attempted halfheartedly to draw back. But German history was too strong for them. *Der Tag* (the day) had arrived—and Germany went to war almost gratefully.

In Paris, on August 2, 1914, thousands cheered the regiments marching off to their mobilization centers; but there was a sober undercurrent to the excitement. France went to war because of her treaty with Russia—but also as a kind of national fate. France was used to German invasions. The last one, in 1870, brought about by Bismarck's cunning and the Emperor Napoleon III's stupidity, had destroyed the French Second Empire and given birth to the German Empire, proclaimed by Bismarck in the Hall of Mirrors at Versailles. It had also given birth to the French Third Republic—and cost France the provinces of Alsace and Lorraine. Since those terrible days many Frenchmen had lived for *revanche*—for the great day when France would defeat "the monstrous vanity created in 1870" and reclaim her lost territory.

But most Frenchmen were not eager for war in 1914. France had a population of forty-five million, Germany a population of over sixty million. Without allies France could never hope to fight and win. That was why France had patched up her centuries-old quarrel with England in 1904 to form the Entente Cordiale; it was why she had maintained an unnatural alliance with tsarist Russia since 1898. Yet even though the French General Staff was confident of victory, French politicians were apprehensive. They were not certain they had a united nation behind them.

French royalists of various persuasions had never accepted the Third Republic. They viewed it as illegitimate, weak, atheistic, and insufficiently dedicated to glory and revenge. In 1898 royalist hatred of French democracy had disrupted the life of the nation and brought France to the brink of civil war. The trouble had been ignited by the infamous Dreyfus Affair of 1894. Captain Alfred Dreyfus, a General Staff officer, had been accused and convicted of treason: of spying for Germany. He had been shipped off to spend the rest of his life on Devil's Island. In 1898, under the prodding of liberal politicians such as Georges Clemenceau and of writers such as Émile Zola and Anatole France, the injustice of his conviction was exposed; Dreyfus had been framed. But French royalists refused to accept the fact that their glorious generals could have forged evidence to convict an innocent man. They accused the "Dreyfusards" of treason, howled that the entire Affair was a Jewish plot—Dreyfus was a Jew—ignited a wave of anti-Semitism, and raised mobs to overthrow the government. The royalists eventually lost—French common sense, French commitment to reason and justice, had eventually prevailed; but they had come close. Would they fight now to defend the Republic they so detested?

And if royalists held a grievance against the Third Republic, so too did French socialists. Their bitterness derived from the fate of the Paris Commune of 1871. In that year of defeat and the destruction of the Second Empire, the workers of Paris had raised the Red flag over the capital. For six months they had governed the city as a commune. But the Paris Commune had been drowned in blood when Third Republic troops from Versailles had stormed the city and then shot down many thousands of workers. Since those days the French working class had regained its strength and its socialist faith. Led by the dynamic Jean Jaurès, French socialists had long proclaimed the international solidarity of all working classes. They would not, they warned, be led to the slaughter of their fellow workers in any insane capitalist war. And now, on the very eve of war, Jaurès himself had been assassinated by a crazed royalist. Would French workers now defend the Republic—or rise against it?

The French government needn't have worried: The tribal pull of patriotism proved much stronger than political differences or socialist theory. The homeland was in danger—and all Frenchmen sprang to her defense.

Germany went to war enthusiastically, France fatalistically, England reluctantly. There was nothing inevitable about British belligerence in 1914. Despite her Entente with France, England was in no way committed to join in the fighting. She faced no German invasion, the ruling Liberal Party was traditionally pacifist, and besides, England was embroiled in her own crisis. This was the Curragh Mutiny, which had been ignited, predictably, by the eternally vexing Irish Question. British troops stationed in Northern Ireland had refused to obey their officers when ordered to put down Protestant rioting against Irish home rule. Generals had resigned their commissions, the political air was heavy with the prospect of treason trials, and a full-blown constitutional crisis seemed imminent.

Yet many English politicians, such as Foreign Secretary Edward Grey, First Lord of the Admiralty Winston Churchill, and the Leader of His Majesty's Loyal Opposition, Conservative Arthur Balfour, understood that Britain would have to fight—for several reasons. The first of these was the traditional British policy of maintaining a balance of power on the Continent. Britain could not sit idly by and watch the rise of any nation to European domination. Secondly, there was the question of British naval supremacy. Germany had begun to challenge that supremacy in 1900 when she had decided to build a High-Seas Fleet. England and the entire British Empire depended utterly—in a way that Germany did not—upon the Royal Navy's absolute rule of the seas. There had ensued a naval building race which had generated dangerous tensions. And finally, decisively, there was the question of Belgian neutrality. Belgium had been the creation of British diplomacy, the child of British policy. The great powers of Europe—France, Germany, Austria, Russia, and England—were all bound by the most solemn of treaties to respect Belgian neutrality in the event of war. Britain could never permit the establishment of an aggressive, conquering power in the Belgian Channel ports only twelve miles from Dover. To prevent that, she had fought Spain's Philip II in the sixteenth century, France's Louis XIV in the seventeenth, and Napoleon Bonaparte in the nineteenth. Well aware of British views, Bismarck had made certain when Prussian armies invaded France in 1870 that not an inch of Belgian territory was violated.

But since Bismarck's day, German plans had changed. Faced with the prospect of fighting on two fronts, the German General Staff had decided to throw Germany's weight against France first, and only after victory in the west (which should come, they figured, in four weeks) turn against Russia. To achieve this quick triumph Count Alfred von Schlieffen, Chief of the German General Staff, had determined to pour massive German armies through Belgium in a wide encircling maneuver which would trap the French armies against their fortress line on the German frontier. Schlieffen was dead before 1914, but his plan was not. Furthermore, its overall pattern, if not its details, was well known to both French and British generals.

But England hesitated—unable to believe that Germany would willingly bring yet another powerful nation into the war against her. It was only when German siege guns thundered against the Belgian fortress of Liège and the field-gray waves of German soldiers poured over Belgium's borders despite the treaty ("just a scrap of paper," German Chancellor Theobald von Bethmann-Hollweg called it) that England went to war. On the evening of her entry Foreign Secretary Grey, watching from a window in Whitehall as the streetlamps below were being lit, remarked to a friend, "The lamps are going out all over Europe; we shall not see them lit again in our lifetime."

To one day relight those lamps was the burning ambition of Woodrow Wilson. When news came of the European catastrophe, Wilson immediately proclaimed American neutrality. Furthermore, he urged his fellow countrymen to remain "neutral in fact as well as name...impartial in thought as well as action." His purpose, he explained, was to enable the United States to "speak the counsels of peace," and one day "play the part of impartial mediator." He expected to bring the gift of peace from the New World to the Old under the Stars and Stripes, "the flag not only of America but of humanity." For a while—a very short while—it seemed that Americans might heed their President's advice.

They followed, in their newspapers, the exciting accounts of battle on the western front; how the Germans battered down the Belgian fortresses at Liège and Namur; of the valiant British stand at Mons; of the terrible French defeats at Charleroi and in the Ardennes; of the German sweep through northeastern France and the Allied retreat on Paris. They read too of the "Russian steamroller" advancing into East Prussia—and of its utter destruction at the hands of Generals von Hindenburg and Ludendorff at the battle of Tannenberg. And they read of the "Miracle of the Marne" when the French and British, their backs to the wall, finally stopped and drove back the German juggernaut.

But that was not all they read. Scanning the dispatches of such superb correspondents as Richard Harding Davis and Irvin Cobb, Americans were horrified to read of German conduct in Belgium and France. In the world of 1914 warfare against civilians was unknown, unthinkable. Yet, as they plunged through Belgium, German troops burned town after town. They took civilians hostage and then massacred them by the dozens, the hundreds, the thousands. They burned the ancient University of Louvain with its glorious library of irreplacable medieval manuscripts, thereby making war upon generations yet unborn. Men, women, children, clergymen—it made no difference; whoever stood in the path of the oncoming German tide was submerged. Nor did the German authorities deny these things. On the contrary, they boasted of them. Every act of German savagery was excused as a "reprisal" for "unlawful" resistance to their forces. Those who wished to dig deeper into the matter could consult the German War Manual, which taught that terror against civilians was essential to speedy victory.

Soon newspapers across the United States flamed with such headlines as GERMANS SACK FIVE TOWNS, CHILDREN EXECUTED, THE MARCH OF THE HUN, WOMEN AND PRIESTS SHOT, and TREASON TO CIVILIZATION. On August 3, 1914, Americans were, by and large, neither pro-Allied nor pro-German; one month later there could be no doubt where their sympathies lay. As United States Ambassador to London Walter Hines Page observed, "A government can be neutral, but no *man* can be."

Despite his deep political and personal commitment to neutrality, even Woodrow Wilson was affected by the German outrages. On August 30 his closest advisor, Colonel Edward House, confided to his diary that Wilson "felt deeply the destruction of Louvain. . . . He goes even further than I in his condemnation of Germany's part in this war. . . . He expressed the opinion that if Germany won it would change the course of our civilization and make the United States a military nation." And even earlier, just after the funeral of his wife on August 12, Wilson remarked in a moment of clairvoyance, "I am afraid something will happen on the high seas that will make it impossible for us to keep out of war."

What happened on the high seas was precisely—nothing. Having created the world's second largest navy, Germany refused to risk it in battle against the British fleet; aside from a handful of surface raiders (soon sunk by the English), the German high-seas fleet remained safely in port. As a result, the Royal Navy was able to establish an ever-tightening blockade against Germany. American trade with Germany and Austria, which had amounted to $169 million in 1914, plunged to less than $1 million in 1916. This loss was made up, however, by British and French demand for American food, munitions, and supplies of all kinds.

U.S. trade with the Allies jumped from $824 million in 1914 to more than $3 billion in 1916. So despite American protests against British seizures of American ships and cries about "freedom of the seas," American businessmen were well content. Besides, every time Wilson found himself having to protest some new British "violation of the maritime rights of neutrals," the Germans would obligingly commit some new act of frightfulness (such as the Zeppelin raid on Liège which inaugurated the bombing of civilian populations) that redirected American anger.

Beginning to feel the effects of the British blockade by January 1915, the Germans determined to resort to submarine warfare. They declared the seas around the British Isles to be a "War Zone," in which Allied shipping would be sunk on sight and of which neutral shipping was warned to steer clear. Often sinking vessels without warning—a flagrant violation of international law—German U-boat commanders began torpedoing Allied freighters and tankers. It was not always possible to distinguish flags at sea and, in any event, the British sometimes hoisted the Stars and Stripes as a deception. On May 1, 1915, the first American ship—the oil tanker *Gulflight*—was torpedoed. Though the vessel was not sunk, three American lives were lost. Then, on May 7, the giant British passenger liner *Lusitania* was sunk off the Irish coast by the German submarine U-20. Of the 1,959 passengers and crew, 1,195 perished. Of 159 Americans aboard, 124 lost their lives. Of 129 children aboard, 94 were killed.

A wave of absolute outrage swept over the United States. It did not matter that the *Lusitania* was, in fact, carrying munitions and other contraband of war; it did not matter that the German Embassy in Washington had published a notice in American newspapers warning against Americans sailing in the liner. The world of 1915 was unused to the indiscriminate slaughter of civilians. American newspapers demanded "reparations" from Germany; some called for war. Indeed there already existed an influential "war party" in the United States, led by Theodore Roosevelt, Ambassador Page, and the influential Colonel House.

Wilson, still dreaming of himself as the arbiter of peace, managed to calm his fellow countrymen. In this he was aided by German considerations of which he was unaware. Shortly after the sinking of the *Lusitania* Wilson dispatched a series of notes to the German government. They did not *quite* threaten war—though they were bellicose enough to bring about the resignation of Secretary of State William Jennings Bryan, a devout pacifist. The notes demanded an official apology, punishment for the U-20's commander, reparations for the lives lost, and most importantly, a German promise to restrict U-boat activities hereafter. It so happened that the German High Command itself was not very satisfied with the results of their counterblockade. They could keep no more than twenty U-boats at sea in 1915—too few to seriously damage Allied shipping. So the Kaiser, eager to keep America neutral, was happy to accede to American wishes. U-boats would no longer attack passenger ships, he promised, and would take great care to warn freighters before sinking them. Neutral ships would be absolutely respected. Meantime, the *Kriegsmarine*—the German Navy—hastily embarked upon a huge submarine-construction program.

There were further incidents at sea during 1916, but Wilson was able to steer his ever-narrowing course of neutrality. Yet war fever was mounting in the United States. This was due, in part, to the cleverness of Allied propaganda. Of greater weight was the booming prosperity Americans enjoyed by supplying the Allies with munitions and raw materials. This ever-expanding trade was now being financed by private American loans—some negotiated by J. P. Morgan, the mighty financier—amounting to hundreds of millions of dollars. The United States was building up a heavy investment in an Allied victory. The influence of the "war party" was manifested in giant "preparedness parades" that took place in major American cities during the spring of 1916. Yet most Americans remained undecided. Wilson was able to win by a very narrow margin the election of 1916 on the slogan "He Kept Us Out of War!"

Hardly had Wilson been inaugurated for his second term, however, before the German government announced the opening of unrestricted submarine warfare on the high seas. Henceforth all shipping, Allied or neutral, would be sunk on sight and without warning in the war zones. And, to accompany this declaration, there occurred another blunder of that Teutonic diplomacy which had left Germany friendless. German Foreign Minister Arthur Zimmermann sent a long, confused telegram to the German Ambassador in Mexico instructing him to propose a treaty of "mutual defense" between Mexico and Germany. The Mexicans were to attack the United States with the object of recovering their "lost provinces" of Texas, Arizona, and New Mexico—California was, for some reason, omitted. British Naval Intelligence intercepted and decoded this idiotic message and offered it to the American press without comment.

In the end, Wilson felt he had no choice. If he resisted the clamor for war his leadership would be repudiated. Yet he hoped that if America must fight, she would fight for something beyond mere battlefield victory. His War Message, which he delivered to a joint session of Congress on the evening of April 2, 1917, declared: "Our object . . . is to vindicate the principles of peace and justice in the life of the world . . . to fight thus for the ultimate peace of the world and for the liberation of its peoples, the German people included; for the rights of nations great and small and the privilege of men everywhere to choose their way of life and of obedience. The world must be made safe for democracy."

And so Americans too marched out of an era. They rushed off eagerly, naively, idealistically, to embrace the last illusion of a believing world: mankind's last great crusade.

> *It was not so much the War as the Peace that I have always dreaded.*
>
> ARTHUR JAMES BALFOUR

2

Anatomy of a Peace Conference

While millions of people in Europe and America cheered, sang, and wept with gratitude at the news of the Armistice, no one anywhere greeted the advent of peace with more heartfelt relief than Woodrow Wilson. Despite his vigorous wartime leadership, he still regarded his decision to bring the United States into the conflict as the greatest defeat of his life. For he suspected that the passions unleashed by war would consume the idealism, the reformist zeal, upon which his progressive program had been based. All the hard-won domestic advances of his first six years in office—advances still bitterly contested by big business and its

Republican spokesmen—might well, Wilson feared, be lost. "Once lead this people into war," he declared, "and they'll forget there ever was such a thing as tolerance. To fight you must be brutal and ruthless, and the spirit of ruthless brutality will enter into the very fiber of our national life, infecting Congress, the courts, the policeman on the beat, the man in the street."

Nor had Wilson ever really reconciled himself to the role of wartime chief. He wisely left military matters in the hands of the military—but found himself constantly embroiled in inter-Allied intrigues. He did not much admire Lloyd George or Clemenceau; he did not trust them to join him after the war in the task of establishing a just and durable peace. "England and France," he wrote, "have not the same views with regard to peace that we have." In fact, so suspicious was Wilson of French and English motives that he carefully maintained that the United States was not an "Ally"— it was an "Associated Power."

Wilson had good reason for his suspicions. For it was now painfully obvious that the English and French had lied to him when they had persuaded him to send American forces to Russia to "protect Allied supplies" or to "aid the Czech Army in its escape." England and France were determined upon nothing less than the overthrow of the new Communist government in Russia—and they were attempting to use American troops for that end. Furthermore, Wilson was well aware of the terms of the various treaties by which the European Allies had bound themselves to prosecute the war—the Russian Communists were gleefully publishing these "secret" agreements from tsarist files to prove how shamefully imperialistic were Allied war aims—terms which carved up nations and peoples without any regard for justice or even wisdom. Believing (rightly) that

"Europe is still governed by the same reactionary forces which controlled this country until a few years ago," and suspecting (rightly) that "French and English leaders desire to exclude me from the [Peace] Conference for fear I might there lead the weaker nations against them," Wilson came to a startling decision: He would go to Paris personally to represent American views.

Startling because until that time no American President had ever left the country during his term of office. The communications of those days when radio was in its infancy, trans-Atlantic cables were uncertain, and no aircraft was capable of crossing the ocean were too slow to allow America to be governed from abroad. Republican Congressmen wondered whether the President's departure might not be unconstitutional; one Senator threatened to introduce a resolution in the Senate declaring the Presidency "vacant" if Wilson persisted. Even the President's friends were against the trip. They feared that once he became embroiled in the horse-trading atmosphere of an international conference, all his idealistic pronouncements would simply sound like the special pleading of an interested party.

But Wilson was still on his moral crusade. "If I didn't feel that I was the personal instrument of God, I couldn't carry on," he once declared. And his self-righteousness was informed by more than vanity: It was based also on the thousands and thousands of letters he had received from Poles, Rumanians, Czechs, Jews, Ukrainians, Slovaks—all the oppressed peoples of Europe begging for his intercession on their behalf. "If you could catch some of these voices," he said, "if you could catch some of these voices..."

Yet Wilson's motives in going to Europe were more complex than that. In the Congressional elections held in November 1918 the Democrats had gone down to utter defeat. The new Congress which would convene in 1919 would be controlled entirely by Republicans— in Wilson's view the representatives of all that was reactionary, oppressive, and intolerant in American life. For the President's fears about the "spirit of ruthless brutality" infecting his fellow citizens had been borne out by the event. Not simply the intolerance that harried Americans of German descent, that forbade the performance of German classical music, that changed the word "sauerkraut" to "liberty cabbage," but the uses to which the spirit of wartime fervor had been put by big business: the brutal suppression of strikes, the judicial murder of radical labor leaders, the unjust imprisonment of Wobbly leaders such as Tom Mooney and the kindly Socialist Eugene Debs—all of this presaged to Wilson the decay of the progressive spirit and the onset of a period of reaction. Repudiated at home, the President might find solace in his overseas role as champion of the world's oppressed.

So, accompanied by Secretary of State Robert Lansing and a huge staff of "experts," Woodrow Wilson set sail for France aboard the liner-turned-military-transport *George Washington* on December 4, 1918. His arrival in Paris a week later must have confirmed to him the need for his presence. For never before or since has any city ever greeted anyone the way Paris greeted Wilson. Hundreds of thousands (perhaps as many as a million) people thronged the President's route to American headquarters at the Hotel Crillon on the Place de la Concorde, screaming their blessings. These huge crowds seemed to pour out their hearts, determined to make the American President the vessel of all their hopes and dreams for the future. The thunderous roaring of their chanted "Wilson, Wilson, Wilson, Wilson" could be heard miles away in the Paris suburbs.

It could also be heard, of course, by French Premier Georges Clemenceau, who officially greeted Wilson. But then, Clemenceau was used to the howling of crowds and inclined to discount it. "I have no illusions," Clemenceau had once declared. Why should he have? He had been a journalist in Florida in 1868 and seen how the recently defeated Confederates indulged in an orgy of lynchings of defenseless blacks; he had been the mayor of Montmartre when the French government put down the Paris Commune of 1871 by killing 20,000 Frenchmen in a single week; he was also a doctor who was made daily aware of the squalor and misery of the poor of Paris. Now an old man, he was seventy-eight in 1919, the Clemenceau who had seen so much was called a cynic.

Yet he was much more than that. As a young man he had been a fervent socialist; his opinions published in his newspapers, *L'Homme Libre* and *L'Aurore,* infuriated French conservatives. And he had risked his career on many a seemingly hopeless cause. He had sprung to the defense of Dreyfus—even helped Émile Zola to write his ringing *J'Accuse!,* published in *L'Aurore,* which broke that sensational case of injustice wide open. Although he confessed to but little faith in that abstraction The People, he declared, "I believe in pity, in the generous outburst of the spirit, in the thirst for justice in the hearts of isolated men." And he believed in France. When called out of retirement to save his country during the extreme crisis of 1917 he answered all questions with the simple statement, "I make war." Politics? "I make war." Domestic policy? "I make war." Foreign policy? "I make war." Always during the struggle, *"Moi, je fais la guerre!"*

And now the man known as The Tiger of France would make the peace—and he would see to it that it was a French peace, American idealism notwithstanding. Napoleon had once described Prussia as "a cannonball." Twice within Clemenceau's lifetime that cannonball had crashed into France—it must never happen again. France could not survive another German war; she had barely survived this one. Security—security at any price and above all—was Clemenceau's aim. To achieve it he had a straightforward program: Alsace-Lorraine to be returned to France; Germany's coal source, the Saar Basin, to be French; the Rhineland in its entirety to be annexed; Germany to be confronted in the east by either a revitalized, *non-Communist* Russia or, failing that, a collection of strong new states such as Poland and Czechoslovakia as a buffer zone; Germany to be kept permanently disarmed; and, finally, the Germans to be saddled with reparations payments guaranteed to keep them economically depressed for generations.

What of Wilson's famous Fourteen Points? One of them established the right of all people to "self-determination." How could you square that with the annexation of huge areas of Germany populated by millions of Germans? And what of the projected League of Nations—the covenant of which was supposed to be written into the peace treaties? Was that not a guarantee of French security? Nonsense! German adherence to the League would merely mean their signature on another "scrap of paper." The world knew how to evaluate such signatures. The English and Americans, who had not been subjected to the *furor teutonicus,* might rely on German promises and wordy ideals; Georges Clemenceau knew better.

Between the extremely opposing views of Wilson and

Clemenceau stood the British Prime Minister, David Lloyd George. The son of poor Welsh coal miners, a "man of the people" who had built his career in the Liberal Party by attacking the rich always and everywhere, Lloyd George was a veritable volcano of Welsh eloquence. He was quite prepared to face both the French Tiger and the American Presbyterian Preacher. But first he had to fight an election at home.

The last general election had been held in England in 1910—elections having been postponed during the war. Now, while patriotic fervor was still hot, was the time to ask the voters to return their triumphant wartime leadership to power.

Be it said to his credit that the fiery Lloyd George— as capable a demagogue as ever harangued a crowd— attempted at first to wage a sober campaign. He wanted Englishmen to consider the problems of economic and social reconstruction with which they were faced. But he was soon made to understand by the voters he addressed that these matters were not uppermost in their minds. What was uppermost was a desire for revenge upon the enemy—revenge for the million dead and two million wounded, revenge for the ghastly German atrocities inflicted upon helpless English prisoners of war, revenge to be expressed in huge war reparations. Lloyd George tried to warn his constituents that Germany absolutely lacked sufficient gold reserves to pay heavy reparations; that German currency would become inflated and worthless; that Germany would pay reparations by simply dumping cheap German goods on world markets, thereby ruining British industries. The voters were indifferent to these warnings. But they cheered when Sir Eric Geddes, First Lord of the Admiralty, promised that the Germans would be squeezed "until you can hear the pips squeak."

Ever the astute politician, Lloyd George hit upon a brilliant solution. The people wanted vengeance? Very well, let them direct their hatred at the very symbol of German wrongdoing, the arch war criminal himself. "Hang the Kaiser!" became Lloyd George's campaign slogan. Thus he profited by the public wrath while directing it into safe and harmless channels. Harmless because, as Lloyd George well knew, the Kaiser (who was a cousin of Britain's King George V) was perfectly safe in his Dutch retreat. Neutral Holland would never, under any circumstances, surrender the royal refugee to whom she'd given political asylum.

So Lloyd George won the election with a handsome Parliamentary majority and went to Paris to advance English interests. Those interests did not completely coincide with either American or French views. Traditional British policy had always been to prevent the rise of any one nation to European domination. This she accomplished by seeking to maintain a "balance of power" on the continent as, for example, between France and Russia or France and Germany, supporting whichever nation was momentarily weaker. But now, of the only three other potentially "great" European powers, Russia was in chaos and Germany in utter defeat. The balance had tilted all the way to France, and if Clemenceau had his way, there it would remain. That Germany must be prevented from ever again threatening the peace of the world Lloyd George agreed; that the way to assure this was by handing the Rhineland over to France, thereby elevating her to permanent European mastery, was unacceptable. As for German reparations, the French and for that matter, his own countrymen might impose them as they wished; Lloyd George privately doubted they would ever be collected.

And what of Wilson's Fourteen Points? One of them spoke of self-determination for *all* peoples, another of colonies "held in trust" under some sort of mandate system to be administered by the League of Nations. Great Britain was an imperial power—the greatest the world had ever seen. Her commerce, her trade, her security, depended upon the maintenance of her empire. Far from welcoming any interference in her vast overseas possessions or accepting any nonsense about the right to self-determination of Hindus, Zulus, Malays, Arabs, and other such "breeds without the law," Britain was preparing to expand her empire, in both Africa and the Near East—in competition with France. England had entered the war as the world's banker and creditor; she emerged from the struggle financially exhausted and heavily in debt to the United States. She would need all her colonial resources and more to regain her solvency and her world trade leadership.

While the decisions of Wilson, Clemenceau, and Lloyd George (the "Big Three") would be decisive in Paris, they were not alone. Also present was Vittorio Orlando, the Italian Premier, who was demanding that the entire Adriatic coast, formerly part of Austria-Hungary, now claimed by the new nation of Yugoslavia, be turned over to Italy along with various Turkish and Greek islands and various hefty slices of Africa and the Near East as her spoils of victory. There were also representatives of the new state of Poland demanding that their nation be reconstituted in her medieval frontiers, which would give her domination over Latvia, Lithuania, Estonia, White Russia, the Ukraine, East Prussia, and German Silesia! There were Rumanian representatives who wished the size of their country doubled—it didn't matter particularly in what direction or at whose expense. Count Makino Nobuaki, representing Japan, demanded that Japan's conquest of German territory in the Pacific and her occupation of German territory in China (also an Ally) be confirmed for all time. And there were Greeks who demanded Constantinople, Czechs who wanted their new nation to include large slices of the German Sudetenland and Hungary, Serbs and Croats who demanded recognition as the new nation of Yugoslavia. There were Russian emigrés who proposed a holy crusade to reconquer their homeland from the detestable Bolsheviks. There were Jews asking that Britain keep her wartime promise, expressed in the Balfour Declaration of 1917, that they be given a homeland in Palestine. There were Arab kings and emirs, each hoping to inherit the rule of former Turkish territory in the Near East. And more.

The only great nation (except the former enemies, Germany, Turkey, and Austria-Hungary) not represented in Paris was an ex-Ally, Russia—excluded because neither Clemenceau nor Lloyd George would deal with a Communist regime which vowed the revolutionary overthrow of capitalist governments. That this omission might, in the long run, doom the conference to failure was not foreseen by the exalted conferees.

Wilson, Clemenceau, Lloyd George, and Orlando held their first meeting in the French Foreign Minister's baroque office on the Quai d'Orsay on January 12, 1919. From the very beginning of the conference Wilson found himself unable to support two of his Fourteen Points. One of these promised "open covenants openly arrived at." But how could you engage in the hard bargaining, the compromising, the rough horse-trading that had to go on with all the world privy to your most private conversations? Agreed—the press would be *excluded* from working sessions of the conference. Another of Wilson's Points had promised that all nations, no matter how small, who'd been engaged in the war or had business before the conference would be heard. But how could you get anything at all done if you had to deal simultaneously with the oratory of representatives from fifty countries? Costa Rica, for example, was an Ally; she had contributed two torpedo boats to the American Navy. Wilson did not approve of the Costa Rican government. "I could not sit at the same table as a representative from Costa Rica," he confided. Clemenceau pointed out that no binding decisions could be made until a conference including all national representatives was convened. Wilson said they should first decide all problems among themselves and then convene the formal conference. Clemenceau pointed out that this might take weeks or months—the delegates of the smaller nations could not be expected to twiddle their thumbs in Paris with nothing to do. Lloyd George suggested that they confer among themselves for a few more days and then convene the conference. Later they all agreed that the delegates from smaller nations should be put to work on such harmless matters as international waterways and the drafting of the various articles of the League covenant. Agreed—important matters would be decided only by the Big Three or Four or Five—depending on whether or not Italian and Japanese delegates were present at plenary sessions.

The third meeting of the Big Five was devoted entirely to a discussion of which language to adopt as the official language of the conference and the expected treaties. Wilson held out for English, Clemenceau demanded French, Orlando suggested that Italian be added. Lloyd George said in that case they might as well add Japanese. Tempers waxed hot. It was agreed to postpone a decision on this thorny problem.

Meanwhile, revolution of a kind had broken out in Germany. The Allied naval blockade of Germany had been maintained after the Armistice to ensure compliance. It would be maintained until the peace treaties were signed. Which meant that many millions of Germans were going hungry—hundreds of thousands were actually starving. Food, clothing, fuel—everything was in short supply. So during the harsh winter of 1918–1919 Germans shivered in rags and fought each other for scraps of food. Everywhere in Germany outraged sailors, soldiers, and workers were organizing councils and seizing local power. It happened in Lübeck, Bremen, Hamburg, Dresden, Cologne, Leipzig, and scores of other cities and towns. These councils ranged from Communist to ultrareactionary—most had no real political substance or program; they were born of acts of desperation and opportunism.

Presiding over this growing chaos was the stunned, frightened government of Germany's new Chancellor, Friedrich Ebert. Ebert and his followers were socialists (whose "revolutionary" demands extended no further than the eight-hour day and health insurance) who had never expected to exercise any kind of power in Hohenzollern Germany. But with the Kaiser's abdication and flight, the German High Command had thrust state power into the unwilling hands of the only large, organized, "democratic" party available—so that a new German government might exist to sue for an immediate armistice. This, the High Command reasoned, might save part at least of the crumbling German Army and thereby preserve Germany from a Communist revolution. The German Republic had duly been proclaimed from the steps of the Reichstag—and representatives of that civilian government had signed the Armistice.

But no sooner had the socialists come to power than they split into factions. One of these factions called itself the *Spartakus League*. Led by Karl Liebknecht and Rosa Luxemburg, the Spartakists were revolutionary Communists of the practical, dangerous Leninist variety. But unlike Lenin, Liebknecht and Luxemburg were not excellent judges of immediate opportunities; they did not know how to bide their time. On January 6, 1919, the Spartakists decided that their time had come. They seized several public buildings in Berlin and announced the formation of a Soviet form of government for all Germany. Friedrich Ebert, who feared and hated Communism as much as any Prussian officer, immediately panicked. He called upon the German High Command to save his government. The High Command, in the person of General Wilhelm Gröner, was only too happy to oblige. But there would be conditions, which could be summed up succinctly: The structure, traditions, and privileges of the Prussian military system were to be preserved in the new Republic. Furthermore, the government was to give the High Command a free hand to pursue its great aim, the preservation of German militarism. To all of this Ebert gratefully agreed, thereby delivering the fledgling Republic into the embrace of its deadliest enemies—for democracy and Prussian militarism could never coexist within the same nation.

General Gröner moved to fulfill his end of the bargain immediately. He could not reply upon his own disintegrating, demoralized regiments—but new formations were at hand. These were the so-called *Freikorps*—gangs of ex-soldiers banded together in armed, paramilitary mobs to loot, kill, terrorize, and thus keep alive the German martial spirit even in defeat. Two of these Freikorps were assigned the task of destroying the Spartakists. They accomplished this with artillery, mortars, and flamethrowers supplied by the High Command—they had their own machine guns. Liebknecht and Luxemburg were brutally murdered, hundreds of their followers killed. Taking part in the action were such later Nazi bigwigs as Martin Bormann, Reinhard Heydrich, and Ernst Röhm. Thus the German Republic was "saved" from Communism. Field Marshal von Hindenburg swore undying loyalty to the new regime.

While these events were transpiring in Berlin, the Allied leaders in Paris were wrestling with the vexing problem of what to do about Russia. Clemenceau, who considered the Bolsheviks common criminals and hated them for having led Russia from the war at its most critical point, still hoped to overthrow the Reds through armed intervention. Certain influential circles in Britain (led by Winston Churchill) and America wholly agreed with this policy. But neither Lloyd George nor Wilson could accept this—Lloyd George because he doubted the continued feasibility of an intervention Britain could not afford, Wilson because he questioned its morality. Both the Anglo-Saxon leaders (as Clemenceau always referred to them) had already made private contacts with Lenin's government through the British secret agent Bruce Lockhart and the American military attaché Colonel Raymond Robins. Both these unofficial observers had reported that the Bolsheviks enjoyed overwhelming support among the Russian people, that the various reactionary generals and admirals supported by Allied money and supplies would speedily collapse once that support was withdrawn, and that Lenin, Trotsky, and their associates were intelligent, reasonable men eager to come to some accommodation with the Western powers. Lloyd George, with Wilson's support, proposed that the Allies invite representatives of the Bolshevik government as well as representatives of the various White (counterrevolutionary) forces in Russia to meet with Allied diplomats on neutral territory. Clemenceau, while stating that France would take no part in such a conference, said he would not stand in the way. A message was dispatched to Moscow.

While they were awaiting the Soviet reply, there was the Polish question to consider. The Poles were one of Wilson's favorite "oppressed peoples." In fact the thirteenth of his Fourteen Points had called for "an independent Polish state which should include the territories inhabited by indisputably Polish populations." Not only had Wilson been charmed by the pianist Ignace Paderewski, who had toured the United States during the war, playing Chopin and pleading the Polish cause; he also recalled that Polish Americans comprised a very sizable bloc of voters. Clemenceau, without illusions regarding the "nobility" of the suffering Poles, nevertheless wanted to see a strong Poland come into existence both as a counterweight to German power in central Europe and as part of a *"cordon sanitaire"* against the spread of Bolshevism to the West. Lloyd George was highly skeptical of both views. He tended to agree with his young advisor John Maynard Keynes, who described Poland as "an economic impossibility with no industry but Jew-baiting." Furthermore, he doubted if a reborn Poland would eventually be able to stand up against Germany, or against Bolshevik Russia for that matter.

But the Poles were, in any event, taking matters into their own hands. An Allied-armed Polish Army had come into being and was driving White Russian and Ukrainian forces out of the country. As Poland had, as yet, no agreed-upon boundaries, Polish military leaders envisioned the seizure of huge chunks of Germany and Russia. They also envisioned the extermination of Poland's very large Jewish population. The disease of anti-Semitism in Poland was ancient and widespread; it infected every aspect of Polish life. Thus, wherever the forces of the new Polish Army went, terrible *pogroms* (massacres; from a Russian word meaning devastation) were carried out against the helpless Jewish residents. At Warsaw, Lvov, Krakow, and a hundred other Polish cities and towns Jewish ghettoes were burned, Jewish synagogues defiled, Jewish shops and homes looted, Jewish men, women, and children murdered. Thousands upon thousands were killed under conditions of appalling ferocity by mobs of Poles supported by the Polish armed forces.

News of the Polish massacres soon found its way into the English and American press. Public opinion was aroused. But without a military force at their disposal in Poland, what could the Allied leaders do? The French wanted to send an army—or create one of Poles, Hungarians, Ukrainians, and Rumanians under Allied leadership. But aside from the fact that these nationalities were already at each other's throats, it was only too obvious to Lloyd George and Wilson that this army's objective would not be to impose order in Poland but rather to conquer Soviet Russia. The Big Three turned to other matters.

The Australian and New Zealand Prime Ministers now appeared before Lloyd George, Wilson, and Clemenceau to announce that they would by no means relinquish control of the former German territories they'd conquered in the Pacific to any League of Nations mandate system. Wilson was outraged. Lloyd George was embarrassed. Clemenceau was amused. France opposed the mandate system mainly because it prohibited the use of native troops from a mandated

territory for any military purpose other than the defense of that territory. But France owed its very survival, in part at least, to the colonial forces it had
rushed from Algeria, Senegal, and even distant Indochina to the Western front. Lloyd George reassured
Clemenceau on this point. Only the use of "big nigger
armies for the purposes of *aggression*" would be prohibited; they could still be used for defense. Clemenceau was relieved. The Australians and New Zealand-
ers retired.

After the modest, sensible, and scholarly Eduard
Beneš, representative and soon to be Premier of the
new state of Czechoslovakia, had outlined to the Big
Three the history of Bohemia since 1526 ("But he has
been such a bore, your Beneš!" Clemenceau muttered
wearily), the Emir Faisal appeared, dressed in flowing
Arab robes. His translator was none other than T. E.
Lawrence, the famed "Lawrence of Arabia." Emir
Faisal, who claimed overlordship in Syria, spent most
of his time reciting the Koran in Arabic to the august
assemblage. Lawrence "freely" translated all this into
a plea for Arab independence. They were followed by
Belgian Prime Minister Paul Hymans, who demanded
Luxembourg and two sections of Holland as compensation for his country's sufferings under the German
occupation. Since Holland had not been at war with
the Allies, it was not immediately apparent how this
claim could be satisfied. It was with considerable relief
that Woodrow Wilson turned to the matter he considered of overwhelming importance at the conference—
the establishment of a League of Nations.

The idea of such a League had many sources. Liberal and idealistic thinkers in Britain and America had
proposed such a scheme long before the Great War had
broken out. Even the bellicose Theodore Roosevelt,

when accepting his Novel Peace Prize in 1906, had spoken favorably of a "league of peace." Private organizations had been formed in Britain and America to pursue this dream. The name "League of Nations" had been coined by Goldsworthy Lowes Dickinson, who, in 1915, helped found a League of Nations Society in London. In 1916 the British government appointed a commission to study the matter. They leaned heavily upon the views of South African Prime Minister Jan Christiaan Smuts, long a League advocate. Wilson refused to appoint an American League commission; he was skeptical of the entire proposal. Instead, the detailed plans of the British Commission were forwarded to him from time to time. These he modified somewhat, rewrote, and presented to the world and to the Paris Conference as his own plan. In doing so he did not fail to warn the amused British not to oppose his plan with some cynical scheme of their own!

The work of the conference committees on the League of Nations covenant consumed Wilson's failing energy resources. He insisted on presiding personally over the task, read all the voluminous reports, and made certain that the final plan was his in every detail. Shortly before this task was completed, Count Makino Nobuaki of Japan addressed the Big Three. Japan wholeheartedly supported the League principle, he declared. He reminded his audience that the world was still suffering from racial antagonisms. There should be no place for racism in the new world order. Therefore Japan proposed that an article be added to the League proposal declaring that its members would accord to all peoples "equal and just treatment in every respect, making no distinction, either in fact or in law, on account of their race or nationality."

Wilson turned pink with embarrassment. United

States immigration laws were based, in large part, on racial discrimination. In California, Oregon, Washington, and several other western states Japanese could not own land; in no case could they become citizens. In the states of the Old South, blacks existed in the peonage of tenth-class citizenship. If such an article were added to the League covenant, the United States Senate would never approve the treaty. Wilson mumbled his thanks for Count Makino's support of the League idea and the meeting adjourned.

By February 14 the work of the conference committee on the League was completed. On that day Wilson read to the conference the final draft of the proposed covenant. Later, while Wilson and Clemenceau were leaving the Quai d'Orsay, they ran into Winston Churchill. He wanted an army with which to invade Soviet Russia to put the Bolsheviks to rout. Wilson stared at him in disbelief and said, "I hesitate to express any definite opinion on this question." An hour later Wilson left for the French port of Brest, where the *George Washington* waited to take him back to the United States.

*What I seem to see—with all my heart I hope
that I am wrong—is a tragedy of disappointment.*

WOODROW WILSON

3

The Light That Failed

The America to which Wilson returned after his two
months abroad was frustrated, leaderless, and savagely
attacking its own vitals. It was as if all the pent-up
emotions of wartime, having now no foreign enemy
upon which to vent themselves, had turned inward. Ir
fact, the United States had gotten all dressed up for a
war—and arrived at the battlefront just as the fighting
ended. The nation's militant energies were taking ugly
directions.

The struggle between big business and organized
labor had been postponed by wartime prosperity. If
prices had gone sky-high from 1914 to 1918, wages had

risen considerably too. And with the United States supplying not only its own armies but those of the Allies as well, with American farmers feeding half the world, there had been work for everyone. With the Armistice this prosperity came to an abrupt end. Munitions factories closed, steel plants reverted to lower production schedules, the entire vast economic machine mobilized for war ground to a halt. Hundreds of thousands were thrown out of work. To their ranks were added the now-returning war veterans seeking jobs. By the time Wilson returned in late February 1919, more than 3 million Americans (10 percent of the labor force of those days) were out of work. Millions of others were working only part time; millions more saw their wages reduced.

All of this was happening in a country with no social security system, no unemployment insurance, no big, militant unions with fat strike funds, no Federal laws protecting workers or even recognizing their right to organize. And businessmen seeking to keep hours long, wages low, and workers disorganized now had a new weapon to add to their arsenal of strikebreakers, hired Pinkerton thugs, and venal politicians—the bogey of Bolshevism. Every time workers tried to strike for better conditions, the charge of Bolshevism was raised against them. Anyone advocating such reforms as child labor laws, workmen's compensation insurance, the eight-hour day, was denounced as a Bolshevik. It was under the cloak of whipped-up anti-Bolshevik hysteria that the one militant labor organization, the I.W.W., was smashed once and for all—its leaders killed or imprisoned, its members blacklisted.

And the lynching of blacks, which had been declining before the war, was now resumed with a vengeance in the Southern States. Black veterans were special targets for mob violence; hundreds met violent death. The long-dead and almost-forgotten Ku Klux Klan was reborn in 1915 at Stone Mountain, Georgia. Its membership jumped by hundreds of thousands as the war ended.

During the war Congress had enacted a Sedition Act (of highly questionable constitutionality) which made any printed or spoken attack on the government a crime. This law was now being used to harry and imprison newspaper editors, writers, filmmakers, and politicians who dared to criticize the wave of reaction. More than a thousand individuals went to jail under the Sedition Act. Following the lead from Washington, thirty-four states enacted totally unconstitutional and hysterical anti-Bolshevik laws of their own.

The nation was leaderless not only because its President was in Europe—but also because in his absence it was being ruled by a lame-duck Congress. The Republicans had won the Congressional elections of 1918. But the new Congress would not convene until March. Meanwhile the House and Senate were still under the control of Democrats who had lost their popular mandate—and their morale.

But Wilson was not returning to the United States to embroil himself in all these distasteful domestic disputes. He did not intend to stay long. He had come back primarily to silence his stay-at-home critics. That these critics, who included representatives, senators, governors, and much of the nation's press, had, in fact, stayed at home was entirely due to Wilson's refusal to invite them to accompany him to Paris. Not a single congressman was asked to join the American delegation— and as for the press, their representatives had been excluded from the conference from the start. But the voices of Wilson's domestic critics were heard across the Atlantic—and were undermining Wilson's authority with the European leaders. Both Lloyd George and Clemenceau understood perfectly well that any treaty agreed to by Wilson would have to secure the approval of two thirds of the United States Senate before it bound the Americans to anything. Neither was it hidden from them that the next Congress would be controlled by the Republican Party and that the most influential Republican in the country, Senator Henry Cabot Lodge of Massachusetts, was making speeches denouncing Wilson and all his works.

Henry Cabot Lodge, the short, silver-haired, distinguished descendant of Boston's two most patrician families, not only detested the President's views, but also loathed him personally. Highly conservative on domestic issues, Lodge had been, in his time, a radical in foreign affairs. He was, to put it simply, an out-and-out imperialist. With the vociferous support of his best friend, Theodore Roosevelt, Lodge had engineered America's war against Spain in 1898. He had led the Senate fight for a huge navy, for the annexation of Hawaii, and for the seizure of Puerto Rico and the Philippines. Later, when Roosevelt became President, Lodge had supported his "Big Stick" diplomacy—as he would later support the "Dollar Diplomacy" of President William Howard Taft. And when the World War started, Lodge and Roosevelt began urging American participation from the very beginning. Not out of any great sympathy for the Allies—all of Europe was a degenerate place to Lodge—but mainly to secure America's imperial interests overseas. Viewing the Allied nations as rivals, Lodge believed that George Washington's warning against entangling alliances with the Old World was as pertinent in 1919 as it had been in 1797. The idea that the United States should surrender any modicum of its sovereignty to some League of Nations was, to Lodge, unthinkable.

Lodge instinctively disliked Wilson's self-righteousness and despised his idealistic generalizations. Nor could he forgive the President for the way he had treated Theodore Roosevelt. When America had entered the war in April 1917, the old Rough Rider had begged Wilson for a battlefield command—a request Wilson contemptuously denied him. Later, when Roosevelt's son Quentin was killed in action on the western front, Wilson withheld condolences. Nor would Wilson divert his motorcade a few miles to visit Quentin Roosevelt's grave in France. This incident shocked Wilson's French hosts and confirmed Lodge in his low opinion of the President's character—and he firmly believed that Wilson's attitude hastened the death of Theodore Roosevelt in January 1919.

Wilson, whose attitude would later be described by Lloyd George as "ecclesiastical" rather than political, refused to play politics with his ideals. He felt himself unable to compromise in any way with his sacred mission. He wired ahead from the *George Washington* asking the members of both the Senate and House Foreign Relations Committees to have dinner with him in the White House. He would, he promised, bring them up to date on his work at the Peace Conference. Meantime they were to make no speeches regarding the League of Nations before he'd talked to them. But as soon as the *George Washington* docked in Boston, Wilson himself made a hot speech denouncing opponents of the League as selfish, narrow, bigoted, and provincial. Under the circumstances, the White House dinner was a disaster. Lodge maintained a baleful silence—other senators and representatives seemed merely embarrassed.

On March 3, 1919, the day before Wilson was to return to Paris, Lodge introduced a resolution on the Senate floor. It stated that the Senate rejected the League covenant as presently drafted and advised the Peace Conference to get on with the peace treaties. He had the signatures of thirty-four senators in support of this resolution. Lodge's motion was defeated as he knew it would be but the world was put on notice that *more than one third* of the United States Senate opposed Wilson's League of Nations. The next day Wilson defended his work in a fiery speech at New York's Metropolitan Opera House—and then embarked once again for Europe.

In his absence some remarkable things had happened in Paris. For one, Georges Clemenceau had been the victim of an assassin's bullet. The tough old Tiger had not been killed ("Clumsy fellow," Clemenceau remarked as he saw his assailant take aim, "he's going to miss me!") but one of the bullets lodged in his chest and rendered him temporarily incapacitated. For another, the conference began work on the peace treaty with Germany. Lloyd George had returned to London to mend political fences and, in the absence of the Big Three, their assistants took over. Colonel Edward M. House, the President's confidant, Arthur James Balfour, British Foreign Secretary, and Stéphen Pichon, French Minister of Foreign Affairs, carried forward the work of the conference.

Entirely on his own initiative, Colonel House, an aggressively optimistic Texan, decided to clear up once and for all the vexing Russian problem. Despite Lenin's favorable response, the Allies had allowed their previous proposal for a meeting on neutral ground to evaporate. House determined to send his own agents to Moscow. After consulting with Lloyd George's private secretary, Philip Kerr, the Colonel appointed a young State Department intelligence agent, William Bullitt, to go secretly to Russia. Bullitt was to offer the Bolsheviks peace and economic aid in return for an end to the Russian civil war and an amnesty for all Russians who had fought against the Bolsheviks. Bullitt asked Lincoln Steffens, a famous American journalist who had access to Trotsky and other high Soviet officials, to accompany him. With high hopes these two departed for Moscow late in February 1919. The French were not informed of this mission.

On February 24, the conferees accepted Balfour's proposal that they concentrate on making peace with Germany first, rather than continue with the distracting task of drawing boundary lines in the Balkans. The French position on Germany's future was clear: France wanted the Rhineland and that was that. Neither the Americans nor the English could agree to this and so, for the moment, progress was stalled.

During the first week of March, Wilson, Lloyd George, and Clemenceau returned to the conference table. Clemenceau laid his cards on it. France could not, he said, entrust her future security to the League of Nations. The League covenant had no teeth in it; without a League army it would be just a debating society. France must have the Rhineland. Wilson explained that the United States Congress, under the American Constitution the only body capable of declaring war, would never agree to American participation in any kind of international police force which might lead the nation into war without Congressional approval. In that case, Clemenceau said, France would only give up her claim to the Rhineland in return for a firm and specific agreement by England and the United States to come to France's aid in the event of another German aggression. Wilson replied that the Senate was unlikely to approve such a separate treaty. Clemenceau said that in that case France might not join the League of Nations. Wilson immediately caved in; France should have her treaty.

On March 22, Communists took over the Hungarian government.

Hungary, a former enemy of the Allies, badly needed a revolution. Her ruling class of Magyar nobles were as savage, racist, reactionary, and aggressive as any group of Prussian Junkers—but they were a bit more clever than the Prussians. When Austria-Hungary left the war and the old Hapsburg empire came apart at the seams, the Hungarian nobles realized they would need a liberal government to "front" for them in dealing with the victorious Allies. So they installed a *real* liberal and pacifist, Mihály Karolyi (the English historian A. J. P. Taylor described him as "the noblest man I have ever known") in power in Budapest. The Magyars then declared themselves a liberty-loving, oppressed people and threw themselves on Allied mercy.

The French would have none of it. They saw to it that Hungarian territory was occupied by Rumanian and Czechoslovakian troops. When Karolyi protested he was confronted with an Allied ultimatum (of which Wilson and Lloyd George knew nothing) to withdraw Hungarian officials from a huge area of his country which, he was told, had been granted to Rumania by the Peace Conference. This was untrue—the Big Three

had agreed on no final borders in Eastern Europe—but
Karolyi refused to comply in any event. On the other
hand he could not bring himself to order Hungarians
to kill, even in defense of their homeland. So Karolyi
resigned, and into the resultant vacuum of power
stepped the Communists. They were the only group left
with the organization and militancy to oppose the Rumanians. Béla Kun, the Communist Party chief, became Prime Minister and virtual dictator of Hungary.
But no revolution took place; there was no time for
that. There was only just time to raise a Hungarian
defense force to resist the encroaching enemy.

"There is at this moment," Wilson declared when
the news from Budapest reached him, "a veritable race
between peace and anarchy." He insisted that the conferees get down to business, and quickly. Lloyd George
and Clemenceau agreed.

A few days later William Bullitt returned from his
mission to Moscow. He was excited and enthusiastic.
He reported to Colonel House that Lenin had agreed
to all the Allied proposals. Furthermore, the new Soviet
government was reasonable and enjoyed the support
of the overwhelming majority of the Russian people.
But Russia was in chaos, her population starving. Allied aid must reach her quickly, if only for humani-
tarian reasons. It was vital that he see the President
as soon as possible. House agreed; he arranged an appointment between Bullitt and Wilson for the next day.
But when Bullitt arrived at the President's residence
he was told that Wilson had a bad headache and could
not see him. Nor would he agree to another appointment.

Although Bullitt could not know it, the President's
headache was very real. He had been suffering from

them for some time. His health had been visibly deteriorating since his return from the United States. When Bullitt expostulated to House about his treatment, the Colonel told him that an envoy's job was done when he turned in his report. The report would now be placed before the Big Three in the normal order of business.

But an American State Department aide in Paris leaked the Bullitt report to the *Daily Mail,* one of Britain's more rabidly anti-Bolshevik newspapers. A hue and cry was immediately raised about dealings with "Communist criminals" who were even then "nationalizing women," etc., etc. The outcry was picked up by the French and American press. Bullitt's report was quietly laid aside. Later, when questioned in Parliament, Lloyd George denied he'd ever heard of Bullitt or any mission to the Bolsheviks. In the end, to Bullitt's mortification, he was utterly repudiated. The only memorable thing to emerge from his trip was Lincoln Steffens's optimistic misapprehension: "I have been over into the future, and it works!"

With the collapse of the Bullitt mission, the American delegation at Paris began to push another plan to deal with the Russians. This involved Herbert Hoover's American Relief Administration (ARA). Hoover, a young, efficient, very cosmopolitan mining engineer, had been delivering food and medicine through the ARA to devastated Belgium. Later his activities were expanded to embrace much of Europe. Why not, suggested some State Department officials, offer the Russians food and medicine through the ARA in return for a truce in the Russian civil war? Naturally there would be other strings. American officials would decide which Russians would distribute the food; American officials would control the Russian railways and delivery systems in the interests of efficiency. Of course the Americans would see to it that anti-Bolshevik Russians played a large part in the program. To put it simply—American food and medical relief for Russia's starving masses was to be used as a political weapon to unseat the Communists. Hoover himself, although a foe of Communism, was determined to keep his organization strictly nonpolitical, strictly neutral. As for the Soviet government, it could not, of course, accept a scheme intended to destroy it. The idea was, for the moment, dropped. And so too was any last chance of including the largest, potentially most powerful nation on the continent in the new European system of international relations.

Meanwhile, suffering from continual headaches and increasing weakness, Wilson pushed the conference ahead. There were now some seventeen committees and thirty-nine subcommittees at work. Decisions were finally reached.

Alsace-Lorraine was, of course, to be returned to France. France was also to hold Germany's Saar Basin, with its vital coalfields, for fifteen years. After that time the local population would vote on its future destiny. France would not receive the Rhineland (which would, however, be demilitarized)—instead, she would receive an Anglo-American treaty guaranteeing her security.

The boundaries of Czechoslovakia were fixed to include some two million Germans living in the Sudetenland. The boundaries of Poland were fixed to include three million Germans living in and around the Baltic port of Danzig and Upper Silesia. German East Prussia was cut off from Germany by a Polish "Corridor" to the

Baltic Sea. Other Eastern European boundaries were also set (see map on page 84). But whether the peoples involved would abide by these boundaries was uncertain. The Poles, for example, were preparing a great Eastern offensive to conquer as much of Russia as they could before Trotsky's newly organized Red Army could become an effective fighting force. Hungarians and Rumanians were battling over choice parts of Transylvania. Italians and Yugoslavs were fighting for the Adriatic port city of Fiume. Greeks and Turks were waging war in and around Smyrna. Even Britain and France were jockeying for imperial position in the new Arab states of the Near East.

To Count Makino's great satisfaction, Japanese claims to the former German Pacific territories were confirmed—as was her right to rule and exploit China's Shantung Province. The Chinese delegate at Paris, Wellington Koo, objected vigorously to this. Count Makino assured the Big Three of Japan's benevolent, even loving attitude toward China. Japan won. When the Chinese (who had placed inordinate confidence in Wilson) learned of this decision, riots broke out in Peking and other cities. The young student Mao Tse-tung was drawn into the protest movement; he and his friends would never again trust any Western power.

The German Army was to be limited to 100,000 men and 4,000 officers. While the total amount of German reparations was not yet finally settled (figures put forward by various experts ranged from $16 billion to $150 billion), a split had been agreed upon. France would receive 55 percent, England 25 percent, other claimants (mainly Italy and Belgium) 20 percent. The United States neither sought nor was granted reparations.

Europe after Versailles

Areas which changed ownership; which were
formed into new states, etc., as a result
of the Treaty of Versailles

The League covenant was agreed upon—with certain American reservations designed, Wilson said, to ensure its adoption by the Senate. The League would have to recognize the Monroe Doctrine. It would have to agree to refrain from interfering in the domestic affairs of any member. It would have to recognize the right of any member to withdraw completely. To the utter dismay of the many Europeans and Americans who had worked hard in committee to make the League more than a debating society, Wilson's reservations were written into the covenant.

The Japanese proposal to include a clause regarding racial equality was defeated by the veto of the Western powers. A wave of anti-American feeling swept over Japan. The Tokyo newspaper *Yoruzu* editorialized: "If America wants war, Japan is not afraid."

On May 7, 1919, the German delegation which had been waiting at Versailles to receive the Allied peace terms was summoned to the Trianon Palace. They were made to enter by the back door and then escorted into a chamber which had been arranged to look like a courtroom—with themselves in the place of the accused. They were given two weeks to study the Allied terms, make whatever comments upon them they wished—and then sign.

The leader of the German delegation, Count Ulrich von Brockdorff-Rantzau, objected to the war-guilt clause of the treaty. "We are required to admit that we alone are guilty for the war," he observed. "Such an admission from me would be a lie. During the past fifty years the imperialism of all European nations had chronically poisoned the international atmosphere. The policy of expansion and disregard for the rights of all peoples to self-determination contributed to the disease of Europe which reached its crisis in the World War."

With a rap of his gravel, Clemenceau adjourned the meeting.

When the German government learned the detailed terms of the Treaty they at first toyed with the idea of armed resistance. But Field Marshal von Hindenburg advised them that while they might preserve their eastern borders against the Poles and Czechs, they could make no defense in the west. The government promptly resigned. It was replaced in a new cabinet shuffle. The new government, headed by one Gustav Bauer, advised the National Assembly, which had been called to devise a new German constitution, that the Allied terms, harsh and unjust as they were, must be accepted. The Assembly agreed.

On June 28, 1919, a Saturday afternoon, two obscure Germans named Hermann Müller and Hans Bell (the only people Bauer could find who would agree to put their signatures on the Treaty) were escorted into the Hall of Mirrors in the Palace of Versailles. There, where nearly fifty years earlier Bismarck had proclaimed the establishment of the German Empire, they signed the Peace Treaty on the places indicated. Their views on the proceedings were not solicited.

Colonel Edward M. House wept when he thought about what had been done in Paris. Self-determination for all peoples? Thirty-six million Chinese had been handed over to Japan, millions of Germans to France and Poland, millions of Hungarians to Rumania, many millions of Arabs to France and Britain. What had happened to Wilson's brave vision of the future?

The Hungarian Communist leader Béla Kun wrote to Wilson: "Blood and smoke, the blood of a proletariat all but exterminated and the smoke and ruins of villages ravaged by war, mark the path pursued by your allies in the name of that higher civilization and love of peace which you proclaim."

Many of the younger Americans at the Peace Conference had resigned in protest. William Bullitt wrote bitterly to Wilson: "I am sorry . . . that you had so little faith in the millions of men, like myself, in every nation who had faith in you."

The conference was ended. Wilson went home.

It has been fashionable since those long-ago days in Paris to blame the defeat of Wilson's principles upon Wilson himself. Certainly he contributed to their downfall. He had a rigid personality, a self-righteous view of men and events. Unused to dealing with equals at a bargaining table, when his idealistic proposals were not at once accepted he tended to compromise them too widely, to retreat too readily. If the good did not immediately triumph, then evil might as well prevail entirely—to Wilson there were no gradations between the two, no halfway houses his puritanical spirit could comfortably inhabit. It is also true that he was abysmally ignorant about Europe, European history, European politics, European interests. He tended again and again to try to understand European motives by forcing them into an American matrix. As just one example— the Polish generals were not the reincarnation of Kosciusko, they were not the democratic liberators of a long-oppressed people. They were semifascist, anti-Semitic military adventurers eager only to establish their own oppression over their neighbors.

More seriously damaging were Wilson's illusions regarding Communism. His feelings on this score were ambivalent. He apprehended the moral authority of the Marxist revolutionaries as opposed to the detestable tsarist regime that preceded them. Indeed he consistently opposed intervention in Russian affairs: If the Russian people wanted a Bolshevik government that was their business. But he feared the Marxist "theology"—feared its spread to the West. And so little did he understand European politics that it was necessary for any interested party merely to label any movement as Bolshevik for Wilson to oppose it. This led him into unwitting collaboration in the destruction of nascent democratic movements in Germany, Hungary, and elsewhere. Of infinitely greater importance, Wilson's indecision led to the exclusion of the Soviet Union from European affairs during and after the Peace Conference.

But in all of this Wilson was more to be pitied than censured. His political ideals foundered upon the rocks of European political reality. The World War had not altered the interests of the European powers. France was still determined upon security at any and all costs, Britain upon the maintenance of her Empire and the recovery of her commerce, Italy and Japan upon territorial aggrandizement. If these goals had to be pursued at the expense of justice, mercy, and the self-determination of peoples, then so be it. It is hard to see what Wilson or anyone else could have done to oppose or even modify these aims. For in the final analysis the World War had not changed human nature. The ancient human motives of greed and fear still prevailed over more humane impulses. Humanity could not live up to Wilson's ideal vision of it. But his memory should be honored precisely *for* his vision and the hopeless fight he waged—it cost him his strength, his health, and, eventually, his life—on behalf of it. Had Wilson's precepts been followed in Paris it is not only possible but entirely probable that there would never have been a Second World War. So in the long run who was the wiser—the American President who attempted to raise the human condition, or those European leaders who simply accepted it, and by accepting it condemned their nations to utter devastation a generation later?

But Wilson did not leave Paris without hope for the future. That hope rested in the covenant of the League of Nations. Wilson felt that whatever mistakes might have been committed at the Peace Conference, whatever compromises might have been forced upon him— all of this could and would be put to rights by the new international organization. Over the years it would correct the errors of the Peace Conference; it would even correct itself, gaining internal strength and external influence, growing finally into a real world government. The League of Nations was the prize he had wrested from the European leaders in return for all his compromises. His next task was to "sell" the Peace Treaty he'd signed, which incorporated the League covenant, to the United States Senate.

In the new Republican-controlled Congress, the Chairman of the Senate Foreign Relations Committee was Senator Henry Cabot Lodge.

It has often been alleged that Lodge fought against the League covenant because of his personal animosity toward the President. This, however, was but one among many motives. Much more important was Lodge's determination that the Peace Treaty be seen as the work of the Republicans, not the Democrats. After all, a Presidential election was coming up in 1920, and Lodge cherished some hope of being his party's nominee. To be perceived by the American public as the architect of peace would certainly not damage his chances. Beyond Lodge's partisanship, which was fierce, were his quite sincere worries that certain provisions of the League covenant (inseparable from the Treaty itself) would supersede the United States Constitution and preempt vital Congressional prerogatives. Lodge was not alone in his opposition.

Irish Americans clamored that the Treaty would bind the United States to send troops to help England maintain her tyranny over their homeland. German Americans particularly loathed the Treaty provisions by which Germany was forced to admit sole responsibility for the war. Italian Americans fretted that the Treaty robbed Italy of her victorious spoils.

There was a considerable body of disinterested opinion which feared that American participation in the League would involve the United States in all sorts of *unjust* European schemes and wars. Would American troops one day be called upon to help put down colonial rebellions in India or Africa? Was the United States prepared to swallow Japan's grab of China's Shantung Province? Would Americans soon have to help the French collect their impossibly high reparations demands from Germany?

There was a still larger group of citizens who wanted no part of any "foreign entanglements," whether for "good" or "evil" purposes. Isolationists, as they were called, felt that the United States, sufficient unto itself and protected by wide oceans, needed no involvements overseas of any kind.

And beyond these groups there was the vast body of American public opinion which, though as yet uncommitted either way, cared relatively little. The crusading zeal which had carried Americans through six years of domestic reform and two years of war was, by now, played out. People were turning again to the pursuits of peace—which meant, primarily, the pursuit of the dollar.

Lodge's plan for dealing with the Treaty had the simplicity of genius. He would offer amendments to it. If Congress adopted these "reservations" then the resulting Treaty would be perceived as his own Republican masterpiece. If Wilson's Democrats refused to accept the reservations then they would have to defeat the Treaty as a whole in the Senate—and its death would be seen as the work of the Democrats.

"Accept the League with the Lodge reservations?" Wilson cried when these were made known to him. "Never! Never! I'll never consent to adopt any policy with which that impossible name is so prominently identified!" The President determined to take his case to the people.

So, on September 3, 1919, Woodrow Wilson left Washington's Union Station to undertake a train trip of more than six thousand miles around the country. He spoke everywhere—in large cities, small towns, crossroad stops, from Columbus, Ohio, to Bismarck, North Dakota, from Seattle to Los Angeles, from Kansas City to Salt Lake City—and everywhere his message was the same. The Treaty must be adopted in its entirety, without reservations of any kind. If it was not, then the world would fall into chaos and a new, more dreadful war would certainly come.

While the President blazed his way west, William Bullitt expressed his views on the Peace Conference before Lodge's Foreign Affairs Committee. His testimony was sensational, to say the least—and highly damaging to the President's case. The still-bitter young man exposed in intimate detail the gross betrayal he felt had been done in Paris. Senator Lodge thanked him politely.

In the meantime the President's health, which had begun to fail in Paris, now deteriorated alarmingly. His wife, his friends, and his physicians begged him to cancel the rest of his heavy speaking schedule. Wilson refused. He was once again engaged on a crusade. And, it seemed to him, he was winning his fight. The people were beginning to respond. Once they understood the issues, they would force Congress to accept the Treaty. But the strain was too much. Between Pueblo, Colorado, and Wichita, Kansas, the President collapsed. The rest of his speaking tour was canceled and his train hurriedly rerouted back to Washington. There, a few days after his return on October 2, 1919, Wilson suffered a severe stroke. His left side was paralyzed, his speech thickened. When, after a few hours, he regained consciousness, he made both his wife and his physicians promise not to reveal what had happened. He feared that if the public knew the seriousness of his condition, a demand might be made for his resignation as "incapacitated" within the clear meaning of the Constitution.

Slowly, painfully, over a period of weeks, Wilson regained some strength. His speech cleared but his left arm and leg remained partially paralyzed. Mental effort exhausted him quickly. For the remainder of his term of office, his wife and his aides shielded him from as much work as possible. Contrary to accusations that Mrs. Wilson had established a "regency" in the White House, all important decisions continued to be made by the President. But while his thought was clear, it had lost its resiliency—only his Scotch Presbyterian obstinacy remained.

The nation, kept in the dark about Wilson's true condition, wasted little sympathy on its stricken leader. The Senatorial machine ground on. It would be unprofitable to go into the details of the intricate battle over Senator Lodge's reservations to the Peace Treaty. In effect Lodge's amendments, though apparently fearsome to League advocates, were actually of little importance. They would hardly have hampered the League's work nor even much circumscribed American participation. They could easily have been accepted without significant damage to the Treaty. Many of Wilson's followers were willing to accept them. But the President would not. Twice, on November 19, 1919, and on March 19, 1920, the Peace Treaty of Versailles came before the Senate for approval. On both occasions it contained the Lodge reservations. And on both occasions it was defeated—by Democratic Senators acting on Wilson's express orders. In fact the President threatened to veto the Treaty if it was adopted in its amended form. Ex-President William Howard Taft privately expressed the outrage of many League supporters at both Lodge and Wilson who preferred, he wrote, "to exalt their personal prestige and the saving of their ugly faces above the welfare of the country and the world."

But Wilson's fight was not yet over. The year 1920 was an election year and, to make certain that the Democratic Party carried on the crusade, he determined to seek an unprecedented third term in office. He was delighted when, in June, the Republican National Convention, meeting in Chicago, despite all Henry Cabot Lodge's carefully laid plans, denied him their nomination. Instead they chose Ohio Senator Warren G. Harding for President and Governor Calvin Coolidge of Massachusetts for Vice-President. Harding relatively unknown (Wilson correctly reasoned), would be easy to beat (he incorrectly concluded).

However, when the Democratic Convention assembled in San Francisco in July, it was soon apparent that most Democrats looked upon Wilson as an albatross around the party's neck. They would have none of him. Instead they nominated Ohio Governor James M. Cox for President and, as his running mate, former Assistant Secretary of the Navy Franklin Delano Roosevelt of New York. Roosevelt's nomination (he was known as a loyal supporter of both Wilson and the treaty) was the only sop the convention would throw the President.

Wilson insisted that the campaign of 1920 must be a "solemn referendum" on the Peace Treaty and the League of Nations. Cox and Roosevelt loyally spoke on behalf of both; Harding and Coolidge made vague noises about the matter which could be interpreted in any way their audiences wished. But the election of 1920, as we shall see, was really waged on other issues. The American people had already made up their minds about the treaty: It was a bore and irrelevant. Harding won easily in November.

After he left office, Wilson lived on in Washington, a frail broken-hearted man despite the consolation of having won the Nobel Peace Prize in 1919. And he received visits from his old friends and antagonists of the Peace Conference: Both Lloyd George and Clemenceau came to pay their respects. Nor did he ever lose faith in his ideals or their eventual triumph. When in April 1923 Lord Robert Cecil, a faithful collaborator of the old days, came to see him, Wilson exclaimed, "We are winning! Don't make any concessions. We are winning!"

Woodrow Wilson died on February 3, 1924. Hundreds of people outside his modest house on S Street knelt in the snow to keep vigil with his passing, the last of the true believers.

I request that my vote be added in favor of the acceptance of potatoes and arms from the bandits of Anglo-French imperialism.

NIKOLAI LENIN

Stabbed in the back. Yes, that's it! We were stabbed in the back!

GENERAL ERICH LUDENDORFF

4

The Outcasts

When Lloyd George later reflected upon the treatment accorded Russia at the Paris Peace Conference, he insisted that he had always felt "that world peace was unattainable as long as that immense country was left outside the Covenant of Nations." Woodrow Wilson had felt so strongly about this that he had written as the sixth of his Fourteen Points: "The treatment accorded Russia by her sister nations in the months to come will be the acid test of their good will, of their comprehension of her needs as distinguished from their own interests, and of their intelligent and unselfish sympathy." In the end, as we have seen, every attempt to deal

with the complexities of the "Russian problem" had
failed. Like the defeated Germans, the Russians had
been excluded from all part in the task of constructing
a new European order. Historians have since concluded
that the punitive peace imposed upon Germany and
the expulsion of Russia from the councils of Europe
constituted the twin great failures of the Allied leaders
in Paris—the failures that made another, greater war
inevitable. Without the cooperation of the two outcast
nations, no lasting peace was possible.

In the case of Germany, it has been suggested that
by imposing a harsh and vengeful peace upon the infant
German Republic, the Allies sabotaged the growth of
German democracy. Time and again during the war
the Allied leaders had declared that their mortal enemy was not the German nation, but rather the militaristic tyranny of the Kaiser and the Prussian autocracy. At Wilson's invitation and in order to negotiate
peace, the Germans had driven the Kaiser into exile,
his ministers into retirement, and Prussian autocrats
into the shadows. They had established a democratic
government. But the Treaty of Versailles cast all blame
for the war and its devastations upon the German people themselves. And since it was republican ministers
and not Prussian autocrats who were forced to sign and
then execute the provisions of the hated treaty, most
Germans blamed the Republic for all their postwar
miseries. Furthermore, it has been claimed, by postponing peace for seven months and withholding support from the Republic, Allied leaders encouraged the
spread of that violent disorder in Germany which persuaded many Germans that democracy was the equiv-
alent of chaos.

But this analysis is only partly correct. Certainly it
was true that the Treaty of Versailles made no dis-

tinction between "guilty" and "innocent" Germans.
"We know the force of hatred which confronts us here,"
Count von Brockdorff-Rantzau had told the Allied leaders when they presented him with the peace terms at
Versailles, "and we have heard the passionate demand
that the victors should both make us pay as vanquished
and punish us as guilty." But was such a distinction
possible? Who, if not the German people, was responsible for the Hohenzollern tyranny? Who, if not the
German people, had so enthusiastically supported the
prewar aggressiveness of that tyranny? And who, if not
the German people in uniform, had waged the resulting
war with such brutal ferocity? True, the Republic as
an institution could not be held responsible for acts
committed before it came into existence. But that Republic was led and staffed by those same "democratic"
German politicians who had, to a man, supported the
Kaiser both before and during the war. If the peace
was to be punitive it is hard to see upon whom, other
than the German people, the punishment should fall.

It can also be questioned whether Allied treatment
of Germany was decisive in undermining German faith
in the Republic. Democracy was a political system with
which Germans were totally unfamiliar; it was alien
both to their experience and to their culture. They
were, of course, perfectly capable of devising a constitution and forming democratic institutions; but how
much confidence they would place in democratic forms,
how much real political content those forms would hold,
was highly questionable irrespective of Allied policy.
We have already seen how gratefully the Social-Democratic leaders had struck a bargain with the military
High Command and permitted the semifascist Freikorps to put down the Spartakists in Berlin as their
first act of office. But, it seemed, the Communists had

not really been stamped out. For on March 3, 1919, the workers in Berlin called for a general strike. The Freikorps were again summoned to action by the Republic's Minister of Defense, Gustav Noske. This time they made a thorough job of it. During the so-called Bloody Week in Berlin the Freikorps blasted, bombed, burned, and slaughtered their way through the working-class sections of the city. More than twenty thousand men, women, and children were killed. This was German democracy in action. Later, after the National Assembly had dutifully adopted a new constitution, the republican government was established in the town of Weimar in order to escape the "radical" atmosphere of the old capitol—hence the name Weimar Republic.

As for encouraging chaos in Germany—of that, one of the Allies was certainly guilty. The French certainly encouraged and supported more than a few phony separatist movements. They secretly set up and then defended an absurd Rhineland Republic; they financed Bavarians, Hessians, and a dozen other independence movements. Of course all of these quickly collapsed— but the French remained unrepentant. They preferred a fragmented Germany as their neighbor. But the basic cause of the political chaos which enveloped Germany from November 1918 to the spring of 1920 and beyond was the war itself. It was the war which had shattered Germany's political institutions, the war which had disrupted German society. Without a complete, full-scale occupation of Germany, it is not clear just how the Allies could have maintained order there.

But whatever conclusions may be drawn regarding the *justification* or lack of it for Allied policy toward Germany, events, as we shall see, certainly condemned its *wisdom*.

As for Allied policy toward Russia—this displayed

neither wisdom nor justification. But in order to fully comprehend the magnitude of Allied folly in this respect, we must go back a bit.

Of all the Great Powers in 1914, Russia was the least prepared to fight a modern war. Her soldiers lacked artillery, machine guns, rifles, ammunition, transportation, and communications; after a few months in the field they also lacked food, clothing, and shoes. Led by a totally incompetent aristocratic officer caste and generals who were sometimes outright traitors, Russian troops perished by the hundreds of thousands in disastrously mismanaged battles. Although they were able to inflict some crushing defeats upon the even less competent Austro-Hungarian forces, they were no match for the Germans. By 1917 the Kaiser's armies had overrun Poland and most of White Russia and were threatening the Ukraine and St. Petersburg itself.

The tyrannical Russian regime which had invited these catastrophes was so stupid, so utterly reactionary, that were it not for the terrible sufferings it inflicted upon the Russian people, it might be described as a black comedy. The Autocrat of All the Russias, Tsar Nicholas II, was a vapid, mindless clerk whose convictions included only his divine right to rule and a hatred of Jews, Englishmen, liberals, and persons cleverer than himself (which meant almost everyone). He was, in turn, largely governed by the whims, superstitions, and fears of his extremely neurotic wife, the Tsarina Alexandra, whose religious fanaticism can only be described as medieval. She, in turn, was utterly dominated by a brutal, uneducated, lecherous, cunning Siberian monk named Grigori Rasputin. These three appointed or dismissed ministers, generals, and officials, called or dismissed the *Duma,* the powerless Russian parliament, massacred striking workers or rebellious peasants, exiled or executed political opponents, issued or repealed decrees, on the basis of personal whim and "divine revelation." This ancient tyranny, different in no important respect from that of Ivan the Terrible, was supported by a police system so vast and complex that when, on occasion, tsarist ministers were assassinated, it was often impossible to determine whether they had been killed by revolutionaries or by police agents.

This regime had, of course, evoked widespread underground opposition over the years. The revolutionaries, mostly of the socialist persuasion, were fragmented among Mensheviks, Bolsheviks, Social Revolutionaries, and a host of lesser parties—but were united in their hatred of the tsar. In the wake of Russia's defeat at the hands of Japan in 1905 (see page 28), the revolutionaries had succeeded in overthrowing the tsarist power in St. Petersburg and Moscow. But the workers and soldiers soviets, the councils that they had established in those cities, were soon routed by the Tsar's armies. Since that time the revolutionary movement had been dormant—its leaders killed, imprisoned, or exiled. But the sufferings of the World War revived revolutionary sentiment and brought it once again to flash point.

By March of 1917 the long-suffering people of Russia, the 140 million inmates of the Tsar's "prison of nations," had had enough. Revolution swept St. Petersburg and then Moscow and then the entire nation. The tsarist regime was almost overnight swept into "the dustbin of history," and a democratic government installed. A mildly socialistic coalition headed by the weak-willed Alexandr Kerenski soon emerged to guide the nation's destinies.

Both the Allied and the German reactions to these

momentous events were determined by the overwhelming fact that a World War was in progress. The Allies would do everything in their power to keep Russia in the war, the Germans to take her out of it. The needs and hopes of the Russian people counted for little in the face of the life-and-death struggle being waged by the Western powers.

Thus, although the revolution had been ignited by war-caused suffering, although the Russian people demanded that their government end the struggle immediately on any terms, the Allies insisted that Kerenski continue the war. Only by promising to do this could he hope to receive the Allied loans and supplies he needed to keep himself in power. What neither the Allies nor Kerenski realized was that *no Russian government of any kind* could hope to retain power unless it made peace with Germany.

The Germans, eager to foster chaos, had arranged for the return to Russia—they crossed Germany in a sealed train—of some exiled Russian revolutionaries who'd been living in Switzerland. Among them was the leader of the Russian Bolshevik Party, Vladimir Ulyanov, better known as Nikolai Lenin, who, the Germans knew, had been denouncing the war since the day it started.

Born of middle-class parents in 1870, Vladimir Ulyanov had been a revolutionary since the day in 1887 when his brother Alexander was executed by the police for conspiring to assassinate the Tsar. Ulyanov found in Marxism the lever he needed to topple the hated tyranny and, as he thought, construct an entirely new, classless society. A man of incisive, brilliant intellect, deep learning, and cosmopolitan outlook (he spoke several languages fluently), Lenin boldly extended and modified Marxist philosophy to suit his own needs.

More important, he created and led a small, highly dedicated, utterly disciplined and ruthless political fragment of the Russian Social Democratic Party—the Bolsheviks.

Lenin and his followers (including a young radical from Odessa, Lev Bronstein, who called himself Leon Trotsky, and a youthful sometime bandit from Georgia named Josef Dzhugashvili, a.k.a. Stalin) had helped bring about the Revolution of 1905. When that had collapsed they had fled into exile aboard. Then came the war.

To Lenin, the idea that working classes could slaughter each other in war was unthinkable. When in 1914 the various European Socialist parties (all members of the Socialist Second International) declared their patriotic support of their countries' war efforts, Lenin denounced them all. He formed his own group of antiwar socialists and spent the years from 1914 to 1917 calling for uniformed workers to turn their arms against their own "imperialist" governments.

The spontaneous Russian Revolution of March 1917 caught Lenin and all the other revolutionary leaders by surprise. Determined to seize control of this great event, Lenin accepted the offer of safe passage made by the German government, even though he realized that it might one day lay him open to charges of "collaboration" with the enemy. But despite his devotion to the Marxist theory Lenin was never a doctrinaire. His thought was pragmatic, his methods practical. When on April 16, 1917, Lenin's train arrived at St. Petersburg's Finland Station, he was confident that he held the key which would open the lock of Russian history.

In the event he was proven correct. As the only Russian party prepared to promise the people not only bread and land but also immediate peace, the Bolsheviks soon attracted a large following. When Kerenski's continuing war effort brought only fresh disasters upon the demoralized Russian armies, more and more city workers and landless peasants (disguised, as Trotsky pionted out, by their army uniforms) turned to Lenin's leadership. The actual Bolshevik seizure of power during those "Ten Days That Shook the World" (as American observer John Reed called them) in October 1917 was swift and, in St. Petersburg, at least, almost bloodless. Trotsky, who was in tactical command of the Bolshevik forces, described it: "The bourgeois classes had expected barricades, flaming conflagrations, looting, rivers of blood. In reality a silence reigned more terrible than all the thunders of the world. The social ground shifted noiselessly like a revolving stage, bringing forward the popular masses, carrying away to limbo the rulers of yesterday."

We have already seen what then ensued: peace with Germany signed at Brest Litovsk, the emergence of counter-revolutionary forces, spreading civil war, Allied intervention, the hesitant, fumbling attempts of Allied leaders to make contact with the new Bolshevik regime.

We have seen, too, that despite the scattered Communist risings in Germany and Hungary, all of which were quickly crushed, the general working-class revolution throughout Europe predicted by Marxist doctrine and hopefully awaited by the Bolsheviks failed to materialize. This meant that for some time to come Communist Russia would face a hostile, capitalist world. Not only would Russia have to defend itself against that world, it would simultaneously have to somehow extract from it the food, industrial machinery, and technical expertise it so desperately lacked.

Putting first things first, Lenin assigned Trotsky the task of organizing a new army to replace the shattered tsarist forces. This was vital not only for the suppression of the various counterrevolutionary armies and gangs that assailed the new government, but also for the defense of Russia against Poland. For the Poles, elated by their newly won independence and led by self-inflated militarists, had launched in February 1920 a campaign to conquer the Russian Ukraine. Their armies plunged deep into Soviet territory.

Trotsky proved himself not only an inspired organizer but also a master strategist. Rushing from battlefront to battlefront in an armored train, he whipped together new military forces—to be called the Red Army—crushed the counter-revolutionaries, and then mounted an offensive against the Poles which by June 1920 had driven them back to the very gates of Warsaw. There the Poles rallied and counterattacked. By August 1920 both sides were exhausted and ready for peace. The Polish-Russian frontier, reflecting the last Polish successes, was established considerably deeper in Russian territory than the Allies had proposed when they drew their boundary lines in Paris.

Nevertheless, by the autumn of 1920 Russia was at peace with the world—the Allied intervention forces had been withdrawn in 1919—and with itself. But how long would the capitalist powers keep that peace? Lenin had long since analyzed the problem. The way to keep the capitalist world off Russia's back was to keep it busy defending its own interests—to go over to the offensive. But in view of Russia's condition, that offensive would have to be political, not military. To accomplish this task Lenin devised a new weapon—the Third (Communist) International, known for short as the Comintern. This was to be an organization of Communist parties throughout the world under Moscow's direction. By propaganda, subversion, sabotage, and political maneuver these parties would stir up so much trouble organizing mass protest movements, fomenting strikes, agitating against governments, and creating rebellions among colonial populations that the "enemy" ruling classes would be fully occupied at home, without the means or energy to attack the Soviet Union. The first, modest meeting of the Comintern was held in Moscow in March 1919. The second meeting was held in July 1920, and by the third meeting, in June 1921, the Comintern was a going concern with tentacles in almost all countries.

So much for defense—but what about Russia's economic needs? These, Lenin realized, could be met only by trade with the Western powers. Trade, on the other hand, meant diplomatic relations of some sort. But how could you wage political warfare against capitalist countries and still expect those countries to establish normal relations with you? Why should the Western powers, through trade, build up the economic strength of a movement openly bent on their speedy destruction? Because, Lenin explained to his incredulous followers, the capitalist ruling classes had but one motive—greed. The prospect of profits to be enjoyed from trade with Russia would blind them to all else. They would eagerly compete to help build the Soviet economy even if this meant digging their own graves.

In this Lenin was both right and wrong. The Allied ruling classes did not immediately rush to do business with a regime they regarded as loathsome—nor were the Allied governments eager, at first, to extend diplomatic recognition. True, Herbert Hoover's American Relief Administration was now (by 1920) distributing food and medicine to the Russian people (under conditions prescribed not by the Allies but by the Soviet government)—but this was no more than a work of charity; the United States government would have no direct dealings with Moscow. The British, though eager for trade with Russia, were prisoners of their own anti-Bolshevik propaganda. No British government that recognized the Soviets could hope to remain long in office. The French remained hostile; billions of French francs had been invested in tsarist Russia before the war to strengthen her against Germany. Now thousands of private French investors were clamoring for repayment. So too were the Allied governments awaiting repayment of their heavy war-time loans. But Lenin had declared from the first that the Bolsheviks would not be responsible for tsarist debts. How to surmount all these obstacles?

First of all, to lure foreign trade and capital, Lenin instituted a New Economic Policy (NEP) early in 1921. This permitted a limited amount of capitalist enterprise in Russia. If that meant postponing socialist goals, it was, Lenin insisted, the only way to get the shattered Russian economy rolling again. Russians, and foreigners too, were to be assured that capital investments would not only be secure from seizure, but would earn handsome profits. As for the tsarist debts— Lenin instructed Russian trade negotiators that these would be *discussed*, endlessly and hopefully *discussed*, whenever Western representatives brought them up. And as for the seemingly impenetrable wall of Western official hostility and nonrecognition, that must be pierced at its weakest point. The weakest point was, quite obviously, the other international outcast, Germany.

German interest in resuming trade and diplomatic relations with Russia was ambivalent. On the one hand the German ruling classes, the German High Command, and the German republican government loathed and feared the Communist ideology. As we have seen, they ruthlessly put down every Communist uprising in Germany. They also feared displeasing the Allies, as they would certainly do by recognizing Lenin's regime. On the other hand trade with Russia was deemed essential to the recovery of the German economy. And a relationship with Moscow, or the threat of such a relationship, seemed the only available means of extorting concessions from France and England. Also, the German High Command, forbidden to manufacture tanks, warplanes, and other matériel by the terms of the Versailles Treaty, which was enforced by Allied Commissions in German cities, was already brooding about the idea of manufacturing such items on Soviet territory.

Early in 1921, Lenin decided to test his theories regarding Western greed. He had already dispatched a trade mission to England, but the Soviet representatives had met a blank wall of indifference in London; no progress had been made. Now Lenin fostered rumors that Russia was about to purchase two hundred railroad locomotives from Germany. The effect was magical. By March 1921 the English had not only concluded a favorable trade agreement with Russia but had also extended de facto recognition to the Soviet regime. This meant that Britain would recognize Lenin's Bolsheviks as the actual if not the rightful government of Russia;

low-level diplomatic representatives could now be exchanged by the two nations, but not ambassadors. A chink had been found in the Western armor.

Voices were at once raised in Germany in favor of dealing with Moscow. If the English could do it, why not the Germans? However, the government of the Weimar Republic, led by President Ebert and, beginning in 1922, Foreign Minister Walther Rathenau, hung back. Rathenau strongly believed that Germany's future lay with the democratic West. But the German government would have to prove that to the German people. Unless the Western Allies dealt decently with the republican government that was not going to be easy to do.

As for the German High Command, it had already made up its mind. Unbeknownst to the German government, German officers entered into secret negotiations with the Soviet military. Late in 1921 agreement was reached. Germany would build armament factories in Russia which would produce tanks, warplanes, and other military hardware forbidden to the Germans. Both the German and Russian armies would share this new equipment. Selected groups of German soldiers would train with the new arms in Russia; in return, they would share their military knowhow with the Red Army. Thus, from the very first, the German High Command found means of circumventing the Treaty of Versailles.

Nor did the High Command abstain from dabbling in German domestic politics. It financed various ultra-Right-wing groups and established a network of spies and observers to keep watch on their progress. One of those observers was an ex-corporal in the German Army, an Austrian-born political fanatic named Adolf

Hitler. He was paid a small salary to report on the doings of various political groups in Munich. Exceeding his employers' expectations the zealous Hitler, who seemed to have a gift for rousing oratory, took over the leadership of one of these small groups and changed its name to the National Socialist German Workers' Party or, in a shortened form of the German name, the Nazi Party. With the help of various ex-Freikorps bullies he thereupon embarked on a campaign to enlarge his following by attacking the hated Versailles Treaty, the republican government which had to enforce it, and the archdemons he blamed for all Germany's woes: the Jews. Although his following was tiny, his seeds of hatred were planted in fertile ground.

For the myth was now spreading in Germany that the German Army had never been defeated in the field. When, for example, General Erich Ludendorff returned from Sweden (whither he had fled in disguise following the Armistice) in 1919, he loudly proclaimed that his forces had been betrayed by the home front. His mighty army would have won, he insisted, had it not been "stabbed in the back." Stabbed in the back by whom? By Communists, republicans, liberals—and Jews. They had brought on defeat, and all the consequences of defeat—starvation, the collapse of law and order, and the harsh impositions of Versailles.

While many Germans may have welcomed these explanations, most were entirely too beaten down, entirely too absorbed with the problems of personal survival, to give them organized expression. They would, for the moment, support the Weimar Republic and see if it could revive the economy and retrieve something from defeat.

But the Allies seemed determined to grant no

concessions at all to the Weimar politicians. It will be recalled that the problem of how much Germany ought to pay in war reparations had been left by the Paris Peace Conference to the decision of a special commission. This Reparations Commission decided that the Germans must pay some $56 billion. The German government declared itself unable to accept that figure— and Anglo-French troops promptly occupied Düsseldorf and other German Rhineland cities. They also began seizing German import taxes on the western border. This, of course, struck another blow to the prestige of the shaky German Republic with its own people. Some concession was eventually made, however; on April 28, 1921, the Reparations Commission set German payments at a total of $33 billion *plus* the entire Belgian war debt. The Germans were ordered to accept these figures or face an Allied takeover of their industrial Ruhr district. The Germans protested but signed the agreement, which bound them to pay half a billion dollars annually plus a tax of 26 percent on all German exports.

Observing all this, Lenin decided that Russia might well profit from the situation. Accordingly, he suggested that all the European powers meet to discuss German reparations, recognition of the Russian regime, *and Russia's war debts*. The French, scenting the possibility of collecting something on their vast prewar investments, responded eagerly. Indeed, the Allied leaders in Paris had foreseen a way out of the bog of tsarist debt for the Russians. They had included an article in the Treaty of Versailles (Article 116) which declared that Russia might, at some future time, present her own bill for German reparations. Now, it appeared to the French and English, a simple solution lay at hand. Russia could pay off her foreign creditors, both private and public, by simply taking a chunk out of the German economy.

The Germans were well aware of the provisions of Article 116 and had feared Russia's eventual use of it. Lenin had, from the first, denounced the entire idea of reparations—but perhaps now he'd changed his mind? When Lloyd George, following Lenin's initiative, called for a general European economic conference to be held in Genoa in April 1922, the Germans were sure the fatal hour had struck. Lenin did nothing to disabuse them. Hints were put abroad that Russia would avail itself of Article 116. But Lloyd George held out the promise to Germany that German reparations would be fully discussed and perhaps the Germans might even get them reduced. So it was with mixed feelings that Germany agreed to attend the Genoa Conference.

When the conference opened on April 10, 1922, the German delegation, headed by Foreign Minister Rathenau, thought its worst fears were realized. French Premier Raymond Poincaré declared that there could be no discussion of *reducing* German reparations. Furthermore, the entire question of German and Russian debts *and Russian claims* would be discussed privately among Allied leaders at meetings from which the Germans were excluded. Surely, the Germans reasoned, all this secrecy could only mean that the Allies were inviting the Russians to take their pound of German flesh under Article 116. When Rathenau tried to contact Lloyd George to clarify this, he was rudely rebuffed. Germans were still considered "untouchables" by their former enemies.

Then suddenly the anxious, isolated Germans received a telephone call from Russian Commissar for

Foreign Affairs, Grigori Chicherin. Would the Germans be interested in meeting privately with the Russian delegation in the nearby town of Rapallo? The Russians had prepared a treaty in which they *renounced* all reparations claims against Germany in return for normal trade relations between the two countries—and German official recognition of the Soviet regime. Despite his pro-Western leanings, Rathenau, feeling betrayed by the French and English, accepted Chicherin's invitation and signed the Russian treaty.

Thus, to the consternation of the Allies, the two outcasts of Europe embraced. Germany became the first of the erstwhile Great Powers to exchange ambassadors with the Soviet Union—and Lenin had pulled off the neatest diplomatic trick of the season.

The German government was now bitterly assailed at home for having signed a treaty with the hated Bolsheviks. Reactionaries of all stripes, including Hitler and his Nazis, denounced "the Bolshevik Jew, Rathenau." In June the gifted and sincerely democratic German Foreign Minister was brutally assassinated. One month later the German government declared itself incapable of paying reparations and asked for a moratorium on its debts. German industry was in chaos, the value of the German mark was falling fast, and German foreign trade was at a near standstill.

During all the rest of 1922, the French and British debated what to do. English Prime Minister Bonar Law, who had replaced Lloyd George, was inclined to grant the German request; French Premier Poincaré was not. Finally, in January 1923, the French acted—alone. They marched their troops into the Ruhr and occupied Germany's primary industrial region. The troops would stay there, it was announced, until the

Germans began making reparations payments. Not only would they stay there, but they would run the giant Ruhr industries, tax the population, and simply help themselves to German reparations.

The German government, unable to oppose the French with force, decreed a policy of noncooperation and passive resistance in the Ruhr. Germans would refuse to work for the French, refuse to pay taxes to them, refuse to obey their orders. Furthermore, as the mark continued its steady decline in value, the German government did nothing to halt the inflation. Let economic chaos drive the French from German soil. The inflation gathered momentum. Soon it cost thousands of marks to purchase an egg, millions to buy a pair of shoes. By the fall of 1923 the mark was utterly and completely worthless. But however this may have thwarted the French, it brought total misery to the vast majority of the German people.

Once again German Rightist radicals felt their hour had struck. The German economy was shattered, German society in ruins, the German people in travail—and the sacred soil of the Fatherland under French occupation. All of this was the fault of the Republic, the Communists, and the Jews. Several German Right-wing parties began plotting the violent overthrow of the Republic. Among them were Hitler's Nazis. Accordingly, on November 1, 1923, Hitler and his followers (including General Ludendorff) attempted to seize the local Bavarian government in Munich. From there they would march on Berlin. They marched—but got only as far as the center of Munich before several squads of police gunned them down and put an ignominious end to their *putsch*. Hitler himself was wounded and later, with several of his coconspirators, tried and found guilty of treason. He was jailed, under remarkably lenient conditions, in Munich's Landsberg Prison. His trial, which he used as a forum to spread Nazi propaganda, had created only a minor sensation. After all, the ridiculous little man with the burning eyes and bland face was only one among so many rabble-rousers who troubled German political life at the time. In his comfortable cell at Landsberg, Hitler decided to improve his time by writing a book which would explain his personal and political philosophy. He called the book *Mein Kampf (My Battle)*.

Certainly neither Lenin nor the Soviet government took much notice of these political gang wars in Germany; they had more important matters to consider. The Soviet diplomatic coup at Rapallo had not entirely succeeded. True, they now enjoyed normal relations with Germany, trade between the two countries was growing, and the German military was helping to rebuild the Russian war industry. But neither the British nor the French had been stampeded into extending diplomatic recognition to the Soviet Union by Germany's action; trade relations with the West were far from satisfactory, and although the New Economic Policy had stabilized the Russian economy, it had brought no dramatic upsurge. The problems of expanding industrial production, nationalizing the land, and how to avert a threatened famine weighed heavily in Moscow.

These problems did not, however, weigh heavily upon Lenin personally—for he was dying. On August 30, 1918, he'd been shot and severely wounded by a Social Revolutionary named Dora Kaplan. He rapidly recovered from that but his health began to weaken. He was obliged to retire from many of the pressures of his office during the winter of 1921–1922. In May 1922, just when the Treaty of Rapallo was being signed, he suffered a stroke. He was to suffer two more before he died on January 21, 1924. Of his death, his bitterest enemy, Winston Churchill, admitted: "He alone could have found the way back to the causeway. . . . The Russian people were left floundering in the bog. Their worst misfortune was his birth . . . their next worst, his death."

The United States, to my eye, is incomparably
the greatest show on earth . . . for example,
the ribald contests of demagogues, the exquisitely
ingenious operations of master rogues, the pursuit
of witches and heretics, the desperate struggles
of inferior men to claw their way into Heaven.

H. L. MENCKEN

5

The Wrong Side of Paradise

The man who took office as President of the United
States on March 4, 1921, very accurately reflected, in
his outlook and character, the postwar mood of the
American people. Warren Gamaliel Harding, as Alice
Roosevelt Longworth observed, "was not a bad man; he
was just a slob." Where Wilson had been intellectual
idealism in action, Harding was the kindly, amiable,
mindless spirit of Main Street, U.S.A. He was an optimistic booster, a glad-hander, a politician without
important convictions. The illiteracy of his speeches
provided hilarious grist for journalistic mills, while his
fatuous dedication to "cronyism" provided a perfect

cover for the swindlers and crooked politicians who flocked to Washington during his administration. Harding was well aware of his own shortcomings. "My God-damn friends," he complained to Kansas editor William Allen White, "they're the ones that keep me walking the floors nights!" And to Nicholas Murray Butler, president of Columbia University, he admitted: "I am not fit for this office and should never have been here."

So, while his Secretary of the Interior, Albert B. Fall, turned over the Navy's oil reserves at Elk Hills, California, to millionaire Edward L. Doheny in return for a satchel containing $100,000 and then leased the oil reserves at Teapot Dome, Wyoming, to oilman Harry F. Sinclair for equally good and valuable personal considerations; while Attorney General Harry Daugherty (himself accused of involvement in various nefarious schemes) attempted to hide these transactions, President Harding passed his time in the White House playing endless card games with his friends, the aptly named Ohio Gang.

Harding was, himself, an honest man—he had not even attempted to hoodwink the American people during the presidential election campaign. He presented himself just as he was: a small-town political hack. It was because of and not despite this that the voters elected him. The American people were heartily sick of crusades, reforms, and foreign entanglements. They yearned for "normalcy." Normalcy meant a government that would not disturb their pursuit of happiness; would not tax their purses in order to finance Utopian schemes; would not tax their minds or consciences with idealistic visions, nor frighten them by harping upon the dangerous direction in which the world was moving. "The War," California's ex-Governor Hiram John-

son observed, "has set the people back for a generation. . . . They are docile; and they will not recover from
being so for many years. The interests which control
the Republican Party will make the most of their do-
cility. In the end, of course, there will be a revolution,
but it will not come in my time."

The transition from war to peace had not been easy.
It had been marked by anti-Negro race riots in Chicago,
Detroit, and other Northern cities to which blacks had
flocked from the South to find jobs in war industries.
It was marked also by strikes and their violent repression. It was punctuated by the explosions of bombs
mailed to politicians, judges, bankers, and industrialists perceived to be the enemies of labor's aspirations.
One such bomb blew off the front of Attorney General
A. Mitchell Palmer's house in Washington on June 2,
1919. Despite the stricken Wilson's plea, "Palmer, do
not let this country see red," the Attorney General,
making use of wartime Sedition and Treason Acts, had
launched the first, original, patented Red Scare in
American history. Hundreds of radicals were rounded
up and jailed on the flimsiest of charges. A radical was
defined as anyone who favored progressive legislation
or spoke out against governmental injustice. Radicals
who were not citizens were first jailed and then de-
ported. They were unceremoniously dumped by the
hundreds and thousands into boats heading for their
lands of origin. The U.S. Army transport *Buford,* nick-
named the Soviet Ark, carried 249 unwilling Russian
and other aliens, including the famous anarchists Alexander Berkman (a Pole) and Emma Goldman, to the
port of Hango, Finland—which was as close to Soviet
territory as her captain cared to come.

Many Americans, fed on a diet of false and mislead-
ing horror stories about the infamous Bolsheviks in

their daily press, supported these measures. "Radicals" were hounded from jobs, from union halls, from local government, from schools and universities. The newly formed American Legion took upon itself the task of enforcing pure, one-hundred-percent "Americanism." It was helped by fraternal organizations of all kinds, business leaders, politicians, and of course the resuscitated Ku Klux Klan. And, as Wilson had long ago foreseen, under the banners of this fervent patriotism bankers, industrialists, and other conservatives were able to cripple and bring to a halt the impetus for reform.

By the time of Harding's inauguration, the Red Scare had done its work and subsided. So thoroughly cowed was the spirit of radicalism in America that the new President even felt free to pardon the imprisoned Socialist leader Eugene V. Debs. He and his ilk were, Harding dimly apprehended, mere ghosts of the past now; nothing was to be feared from them or from the movements they represented. The pendulum of American politics had swung far to the Right and would stay there for a long time. Other ghosts were also laid to rest. The American people, in electing Harding over Cox and Roosevelt, had signified their total rejection of the Treaty of Versailles. The United States would not be a party to that treaty—which meant that the United States rejected membership in the League of Nations and refused to ratify any security treaty with France. It also meant that the United States was still legally at war with Germany. This was corrected by a separate peace treaty that did little more than proclaim the end of hostilities and that treaty became effective on November 11, 1921.

So much for extricating the country from European affairs—but what about the Pacific and Asia? Which, in 1921, was to say, What about China and Japan? Japanese expansion at Chinese expense was an old and, to many Americans, alarming story. And Japanese conduct during the World War gave new grounds for fear. She had seized Germany's share of China and seemed unwilling to relinquish it. For reasons both commercial and sentimental, Americans had long regarded China as their adopted Asiatic ward. A public opinion which was indifferent to aggressions committed elsewhere was easily and touchily aroused by Japanese assaults on China. And, although American forces had long since been withdrawn, a Japanese intervention army remained in Soviet Siberia. What were they plotting there? Furthermore, at Paris, Japan had been granted mandates over several ex-German Pacific island groups. If those islands were fortified they would constitute a real threat to America's tenuous communications with the Philippines. Also there was the fact that Japan enjoyed a treaty of mutual assistance with Great Britain—in the event of war, that could prove embarrassing. And finally, there was native American racism to consider. The Japanese were a "Yellow Peril" (the phrase had been coined by Kaiser Wilhelm II) which America kept from her shores by discriminatory legislation. Even the Supreme Court had declared that since no Japanese could be considered "a free white man," no Japanese could become a citizen.

For obvious reasons, Pacific problems were inextricably intertwined with naval strategy. It was not merely to defeat Germany that the United States had, during the war, embarked upon a huge program of naval expansion. When and if completed, that program would give Americans the world's largest navy by far. Many of the new ships were still on the ways, others afloat but unfinished. But Americans did not want a huge navy. To complete it would cost hundreds of millions of tax dollars; to maintain it would cost hundreds of millions more. Congress, under tremendous pressure to cut taxes, wanted out. The Harding administration saw a chance to kill two birds with one stone.

Accordingly, during the summer of 1921, invitations were extended to England, France, Japan, and Italy to confer in Washington about general disarmament. To the United States (and England) this really meant naval disarmament, since neither power maintained large, or even adequate, land forces. Indeed, Congress had already cut back the United States Army to 175,000 officers and men. The English, also weary of the tax burden of ever-expanding fleets, were happy to accept the American invitation. The French and Italians, although warning that they would discuss no limitations upon their land forces, were also willing to talk—especially since they had no large naval armaments. Japanese motives in accepting Harding's invitation were, as we shall later see, more complex. And so, on the third anniversary of the Armistice, and the same day America declared peace with Germany, the Washington Conference opened.

It was soon apparent that a bargain could be struck. Japan was willing to withdraw from both Soviet Siberia and China's Shantung Province. She was also willing to give up her treaty with England. She was even willing to swallow her martial pride and accept permanent naval inferiority to the United States and Britain. But in return for all this, the British and Americans were required to promise not to establish or fortify any new military or naval bases in the Pacific or Far East. The British were to limit their fortifications to Singapore, the Americans to Hawaii. Furthermore, the Anglo-Americans were to confirm the Japanese mandate over the ex-German Pacific islands, and no notice was to be taken of Japanese activities there. In effect, Japan was offering to behave herself provided the United States and Britain made themselves defenseless in the Orient and Western Pacific. To this the Western powers were happy to agree. As for naval armaments, it soon became apparent that agreement could be reached on limiting the numbers of battleships and the tonnage (not the numbers) of heavy cruisers. A ratio of strength was set at $5 : 5 : 3 : 1.75 : 1.75$. These arcane numbers meant only that for every five English or American battleships, the Japanese could have three, Italy and France one and three quarters each. Cruisers were limited to 10,000 tons. Nothing effective was done about destroyers, submarines, or the still-experimental aircraft carriers. The Washington agreements were signed on February 6, 1922, and the delegates went home. The British, whose Royal Navy was just about as large as the treaty permitted, had little to do; the Japanese, French, and Italians, whose fleets were below treaty limitations, immediately began to construct warships. The Americans, overjoyed to be rid of an expensive naval building program, promptly proceeded to scrap, sink, and otherwise dispose of what would have been the world's newest and most powerful fleet. The United States could now happily forget that any other hemisphere existed.

The American people, now retired from the world stage, had much to interest and excite them at home. A flood of new inventions (some not so new, but now commercialized for the first time) was creating entire new industries. Automobiles, once the playthings of the rich, were now pouring from Detroit at prices most could afford; the infant motion-picture industry was entering its golden age of expansion and profits; radio was no longer a hobby, but becoming a vast national enterprise; commercial advertising was suddenly respectable and booming; aviation had moved from stunt flying to the beginnings of sober commerce. And these new industries stimulated demand and growth in many other fields. Even the Wall Street Stock Exchange, once the mysterious preserve of the very wealthy, began to attract middle-class investors. After a brief end-of-the-war recession of 1919–1921, the nation entered upon an era of unprecedented prosperity.

The burning political issue of the "Roaring Twenties" turned out to be Prohibition. The Eighteenth Amendment to the Constitution, which prohibited the manufacture, import, sale, or consumption of alcoholic beverages, had been ratified by the necessary thirty-six states on January 16, 1919. It became operative in January 1920 and millions of throats went dry. A last attempt by rural America to impose its tastes and Fundamentalist mores upon an increasingly urban society, Prohibition proved unenforceable in the cities. But like everything else in those years, it too gave rise to a new industry—bootlegging. If Americans wanted to drink, a new breed of war-trained gangsters would provide them with "booze" smuggled in from abroad or manufactured in bathtubs. A wave of criminal violence broke over the nation as rival gangs fought for control of lucrative territories with pistols, bombs, and Thompson submachine guns. Glamorized by cynical public opinion, bootleggers openly bribed local police, Federal agents, and even judges—thereby creating a climate of contempt for law and justice.

Warren G. Harding may dimly have been aware that this contempt had penetrated his own cabinet as he prepared, in the summer of 1923, to make a western tour which would carry him all the way to Alaska. But the disgraceful uproar which was soon to be known as the Teapot Dome Scandal (the Watergate of its day) never touched him. For on August 3, 1923, while resting in San Francisco after a bout of ptomaine poisoning received in Seattle, Warren G. Harding died. As his wife—he called her The Duchess—murmured later to his flag-draped coffin in the East Room of the White House, "No one can hurt you now, Warren."

And so the Vermont Yankee, Vice-President Calvin Coolidge, was unexpectedly catapulted into the seat of power. A slim, colorless, tight-lipped individual of dry personality but unimpeachable "character," Coolidge provided a total contrast to his glad-handing predecessor. Firmly believing that that government is best which governs least, "Silent Cal," as he was called, spent a good part of his time in the White House sleeping. His working day was brief—and during it he often napped, feet propped up on his desk in the Oval Office. If Coolidge believed in anything (and he did) it was business, not government. "The business of America," he declared, "is business." Business was even divine: "The man who builds a factory," he wrote, "builds a temple. . . . The man who works there worships there." Government existed only to serve business: "The law that builds up the people is the law that builds up industry," he observed. As for that silence which became as famous as Babe Ruth's batting average, Rudolph Valentino's profile, Theda Bara's provocative eyes, Al Capone's murderous efficiency, or Henry Ford's anti-Semitic opinions—that was policy. "The things I don't say," he once remarked, "never get me into trouble."

Coolidge moved fast to clean up the government after Teapot Dome, and his efficiency, opinions, and Sphinx-like silence were rewarded when he won the

Presidential election of 1924. His simple devotion to wealth made him the perfect symbol to preside over the wild national pursuit of prosperity.

Many prosperous, articulate people would one day look back wistfully upon the twenties as a golden age. Yet the great national prosperity of those years was remarkably ill distributed. The twenties, to a cold eye, were not only or even primarily the years of gay "flappers," garish "speakeasies," bathtub gin, wild parties, Florida real-estate booms, motion-picture idols, new gadgets, stock-market profits, and limitless industrial expansion. They were also the years of hundreds of ferocious lynchings of Negroes in the South, the years during which American farmers rarely saw a profit, the years when child labor still flourished so that eight-year-old workers labored twelve hours a day in New Jersey cranberry bogs for $4.35 a week, the years when steel and auto workers labored sixty-hour weeks for $15.50, the years when every attempt to organize trade unions was met by Pinkerton violence, Federal court injunctions, and a Supreme Court decree that unions could be prosecuted under antitrust law because they fit the definition as "monopolies in restraint of trade." During those golden years of the Roaring Twenties, the great majority of Americans lived on the edge of poverty—a substantial number lived below it. And those were days when all the benefits of welfare and social security were unknown. The young enjoyed no legal protection against vicious exploitation, the indigent had to depend on fitful private charity, and for the old there was only the prospect of the poorhouse.

Not that Wilsonian idealism or the liberal philosophy were completely dead in America. The banner of reform was still carried—by the La Follette brothers of Wisconsin, by Hiram Johnson of California, by

George Norris, Senator from Nebraska, by Al Smith, Governor of New York, by Supreme Court Justice Louis Brandeis, by various university professors such as Rexford G. Tugwell at Columbia, Felix Frankfurter at Harvard, and Paul H. Douglas at Chicago, and many others, including the defeated vice-presidential nominee of 1920, Franklin D. Roosevelt, although a crippling attack of poliomyelitis in 1921 had, for the moment, undermined his effectiveness. That the spirit of adventure and the longing for an ideal in which they could believe were not totally lost among the people was proven by their hysterical adulation of Charles Lindbergh when, in 1927, the Lone Eagle made his daring solo flight across the Atlantic. That completely noncommercial, utterly unprofitable, absolutely "clean" triumph of courage, ingenuity, and faith was hailed as the heroic achievement of the age.

Yet, as Coolidge observed, the business of America remained business. And not surprisingly, American interest in foreign affairs during the twenties centered almost exclusively upon the recovery of the monies the United States had lent the Allies during the war. The entire question was vexing, complicated, and acrimonious. It was also involved in the complexities of German reparations. In brief, the United States had advanced some $10 billion to the European Allies during the World War—and wanted it back, with interest. But the Allies argued that since the struggle against Germany had been a common effort, and since the United States had suffered no damage and few casualties, the American loans should be regarded as her contribution to victory. Furthermore, it was pointed out, the Allies had spent a much larger sum purchasing war matériel in the United States and she should be satisfied with the great wealth and prosperity this had brought her. Finally, the Allies explained that they could never hope to repay this large amount unless they were free to sell goods in the United States. But, at the behest of American businessmen, the American government had erected and maintained a tariff wall that effectively shut foreign goods out of the country.

To all such arguments and pleas Calvin Coolidge returned the single, grim question: "They hired the money, didn't they?"

Now it was not hidden from the United States that English and French repayment of their wartime loans would probably depend on how much money they, in turn, could extract in German reparations. For this reason, although the United States made no financial claims against Germany, Americans became involved in the tortuous, endless, frustrating question of how to squeeze fiscal blood from the German turnip.

So when, in October 1923, in order to get the French out of their Ruhr the Germans announced their readiness to resume reparations payments, the Allied committee appointed to consider the matter was headed by an American, former Brigadier General Charles G. Dawes. The so-called Dawes Plan which emerged from this committee rescheduled German reparations payments in intricate ways. The Germans began to pay, the French left the Ruhr, and Charles Dawes ran with Coolidge to become, in 1925, Vice-President of the United States.

For a few years the Dawes Plan worked. But it worked in the following fascinating way: American banks, such as J. P. Morgan's, the Chase National, and others, lent vast sums of money to the German government, purchased large numbers of German bonds, and invested heavily in German private industry. The Germans used this money to make reparations payments to France and England. The French and English, in turn, made payments on their war debts to the United States. Thus the Americans paid themselves.

But while the Dawes Plan determined the schedule of German payments it said nothing about their overall amount. That was still fixed at $33 billion by the Versailles Treaty. Accordingly, in 1928–1929 a new committee was established to consider this question. It too was headed by an American, lawyer Owen D. Young. After months of wrangling, the Young Plan emerged. It established Germany's reparations at a total of some $9 billion to be paid over a period of fifty-nine years. In the long run Germany paid almost none of this money; England, France, and the other European Allies (with the exception of Finland) defaulted on their debts to the United States; and worldwide depression soon engulfed everyone anyhow, thereby putting an end to the futile and ignoble haggling over money.

In any event, American interest in war debts and reparations was slight in 1928—for that was a presidential election year. Calvin Coolidge had already declared, "I do not choose to run." Much to the President's surprise and mortification, the Republican Party took him seriously; they nominated his Secretary of Commerce, Herbert Hoover, for the presidency. Hoover's opponent was Democrat Al Smith. Republicans expected an easy victory at the polls. Smith's party was divided, his accent was uncompromisingly Lower East Side New York, he was flagrantly opposed to Prohibition, and, worst of all—he was a *Catholic*.

Hoover, on the other hand, was an eminently safe and sound candidate. All Americans recalled his highly efficient, very successful captaincy of the American Relief Administration which had fed millions of hapless Europeans during and after the war. And they knew him to be dedicated to dynamic capitalism. Where Harding and Coolidge had merely worshipped at the shrine of business, Hoover was seen as its hyperactive high priest. He would use government in a positive, efficient way to advance business interests. Before the war he had been one of the world's most successful engineers; now he would engineer permanent prosperity.

The Republican candidate did have some drawbacks. He lacked Smith's sense of humor, his phrase-coining ability, his capacity for warm, personal relations, his obvious identification with the "common man." In truth, Hoover was a distant, reserved sort of person with a frigid personality. Today it would be said that he utterly lacked charisma. And just as he was incapable of close individual relationships, so too he was incapable of ingratiating himself with the crowd. In fact he despised the crowd. "The crowd only feels: it has no mind of its own which can plan. The crowd is credulous, it destroys, it consumes, it hates, and it dreams—but it never builds," he wrote.

Nonetheless, Hoover won as predicted. Al Smith, the Happy Warrior, as Franklin D. Roosevelt described him during the Democratic Convention, went down before a tidal wave of ignorance, fear, and hate. He was abandoned by rural America because of his alliance with the Demon Rum; he lost the normal Democratic big-city constituency because no one could deny Republican prosperity; he lost the usually Democratic Solid South because of a scurrilous campaign of slander which convinced Protestant America that Smith was planning to install the Pope in the White House and introduce the horrors of the Holy Inquisition to Washington.

When Hoover was inaugurated, on March 4, 1929,

America rejoiced that universal and eternal prosperity was now assured. Industry, protected from foreign competition by an insurmountable tariff wall, was ever-expanding. Business profits continued to climb. That barometer of the nation's economic health, the Wall Street Stock Exchange, rose and rose to dizzying heights. To those who pointed out that American workers were not receiving anything like a fair share of all this wealth, it was said that as riches "trickled down from the top," their lot would speedily improve. To those who fretted about continuing depression among the nation's farmers, Coolidge had given the answer: "Farmers have never made much money. I don't think there's anything anyone can do about that."

As for foreign affairs—the country took little notice of events overseas. The Italians had saddled themselves with a new dictator, a sort of socialist Godfather named Benito Mussolini who apparently made the rich pay their taxes. The Weimar Republic in Germany seemed secure, despite the abuse heaped upon it by that ridiculous Arthur, Aloysius, or Adolf Hitler—no one was quite sure of his name. The Japanese were still making trouble in China, but nothing very serious. As for the Bolsheviks—everyone knew that their rule had brought Russia to total ruin. The best way to deal with them was the American way: by neither recognizing nor entertaining any relations whatsoever with their Godless regime.

"We in America today," Hoover assured the nation, "are nearer to the final triumph over poverty than ever before in the history of any land. . . . We shall soon with the help of God be in sight of the day when poverty will be banished from this nation." Nothing else mattered.

It is my belief that Heaven has chosen Japan as the champion of the East.

OKAWA SHUMEI

The Philippines not contiguous? American speed, American guns, American heart and brain and nerve will keep them contiguous forever!

SENATOR ALBERT BEVERIDGE

6

Pacific Overtures

While the years of "prosperity" passed, all but unnoticed in the United States, a slow, deadly fuse was sputtering in the Orient. And since most Americans today are little better informed about Far Eastern history than they were in the twenties, it may be useful to trace that fuse to an earlier time than has seemed necessary for the better-known history of Europe. We can, in fact, identify the exact day on which it was ignited. . . .

When, on July 8, 1853, the Western barbarian Commodore Matthew Calbraith Perry furled the sails of his four black warships (a paddle-wheel frigate and three sloops) against the sky above Edo (Tokyo) Bay, he raised the curtain on a drama which, with all the deadly inevitability of Greek tragedy, moved unswervingly to a shattering climax in the sky above Pearl Harbor some eighty-eight years later. Yet neither Perry nor any subsequent American emissaries, ambassadors, or politicians ever intended such a denouement; they acted almost entirely through ignorance. For this ignorance they could be excused at first, for Japan (or, as the Japanese called it, Nippon) was indeed a mysterious place.

The Portuguese, Spaniards, Dutch, and English knew something of these North Pacific islands. During the sixteenth and seventeenth centuries they had traded with their short, yellow-hued inhabitants, largely through the port of Nagasaki. European sailing vessels frequently called there for repairs and replenishment as well as trade. Christian missionaries (Jesuits and Franciscans) were even permitted to live in Japan and preach their religion. But as the Japanese ruling classes slowly began to realize that they were being cheated by Western merchants, that these same merchants often carried off Japanese children to be sold elsewhere into slavery, and that the Christian missionaries were preaching a doctrine which roused Japan's peasantry against their feudal overlords, these early Western contacts were brought to a speedy and grisly end. Jesuit and Franciscan priests were executed by the dozens, their followers massacred by the thousands, and Japan officially closed to any and all ships from abroad. All this had transpired some two hundred years before Perry's arrival. During those two centuries Japan kept interlopers away—and woe betide the crew of any foreign vessel unlucky enough to be shipwrecked on her shores.

And in fact American ships—the tubby North Pacific whalers and the sleek, swift China Clippers—often came to grief in Japanese waters. Since American expansion to the Pacific during the 1840s, American trade with China (a trade older than the United States) had greatly expanded. It was vital that American ships be able to shelter in Japanese harbors during storms, that they be able to water and refit in Japanese ports, that if wrecked on Japanese shores their crews not be killed out of hand. It was to secure these simple privileges and, possibly, even negotiate a trade treaty that President Millard Fillmore had dispatched Commodore Perry's small flotilla. He had even given Perry a personal letter from himself to the Mikado, the Japanese Emperor. Aware that a previous American expedition under Commodore James Biddle in 1846 had failed to achieve these same purposes, Commodore Perry set about learning all he could of Japanese ways and manners before he set sail. The Japanese were, he decided, a people much given to ceremony and ritual, and a people of proud warrior traditions. So by combining elaborate ceremony, strict attention to Japanese rituals, and a plain and threatening show of force, Commodore Perry succeeded in delivering his letter—if not to the Emperor, at least to a prince of the royal blood. He said he would return in one year for an answer.

Perry's visit provoked an uproar among the Japanese ruling class. The governing power with which the American Commodore had actually dealt was not the Imperial Court but rather the *Bakufu*—a name translated literally as "camp government." That definition very aptly describes the Bakufu's origins. It had been established as a military regime by the warlord Yoritomo in 1192 after many decades of civil war and social chaos. Ever since that time the Bakufu had been dominated by one or another of Japan's warlord families, with the help of the *daimyo* (local lords) and the support of that special military order known as the *samurai* (warriors). The head of the Bakufu was called the *shogun*—the military commander in chief of the entire nation. Of course the Bakufu, the daimyo, the samurai, and the shogun himself owed allegiance and obedience to the Emperor. But despite the fact that the Mikado could trace his ancestry back to the Sun-Goddess herself and was therefore divine, he had, since the beginning of the thirteenth century, exercised no real power. The Emperor was revered—but Japan was run entirely by the Bakufu, not the Imperial Court.

The basic problem faced by Japan's ruling classes after Perry's visit was their apprehension that opening Japan to Western influences would inevitably undermine their own semifeudal power, privileges, and position. For more than a thousand years they had maintained themselves by the ruthless exploitation of the masses of the Japanese peasantry. It was to keep those masses in ignorance, to keep them docile and enthralled, that Japan's warrior nobles had sealed their island nation from all contact with the outside world. But now, as a result of that policy, Japan lacked the modern weapons and technology to preserve itself against foreign intrusion.

No sooner had Perry's "black ships" sailed away than an uproar of conflicting advice descended upon the Bakufu. Some daimyo advocated that the policy of exclusion be maintained but war avoided, a clearly impossible position. Others, like the Daimyo of Mito, Tokugawa Nariaki, advised all-out resistance. After all, had not the great thinker Aizawa Seishisai written back in 1825, "Today the alien barbarians of the West, lowly organs of the legs and feet of the world, are dashing about across the sea, trampling other countries underfoot and daring, with their squinting eyes and limping feet, to override the noble nations. What manner of arrogance is this! . . . Our Divine Land is situated at the top of the earth. . . . It [America] occupies the hindmost regions of the world; thus, its people are stupid and simple, and are incapable of doing things." But by 1853 even the obdurate Tokugawa Nariaki had to sadly admit, "In these feeble days men tend to cling to peace; they are not fond of defending their country by war."

When Commodore Perry returned as promised (this time with *eight* of the terrible "black ships") the Bakufu saw no other course but to accept the American proposals. By the Treaty of Kanagawa, signed on March 31, 1854, the Bakufu agreed to open two ports (Hakodate and Shimoda) to American vessels, to treat shipwrecked sailors properly, and to accept an American consul in Shimoda. The first of these, Townsend Harris, concluded a commercial treaty with the Bakufu in 1856. Following the American lead, England, France, Russia, and Holland soon wrested similar treaties from the reluctant Bakufu. By 1860, when the first Japanese embassy was dispatched to Washington, Japan was open to the rest of the world.

But many daimyo refused to accept this reality. They rallied against the Bakufu through the Imperial Court and the Mikado Komei. Hatred of foreigners, fanatical patriotism, and reverence for the Emperor were the three threads of their policy. Woven together, these threads provided a rope strong enough to hang the Bakufu. After a series of political assassinations, riots, and military skirmishes which did not quite amount to civil war, the last shogun, Tokugawa Hitotsubashi Yoshinobu, renounced his position and dissolved the

Bakufu. Henceforth real political power in Japan would be wielded by the Imperial Court. Komei died in 1867 and in 1869 the young Mikado Meiji established his imperial government in Edo, now renamed Tokyo, and a new era began. It was to be one of the most remarkable in the history of any nation.

With a ruthlessness possible only to an absolutist regime, the Meiji government embarked upon a swift, wholesale modernization of the entire nation. It proceeded to dismantle Japan's ancient feudal system by buying up the estates of the daimyo. The land was then offered for sale in small parcels to whoever could afford to buy it. The daimyo and the samurai were organized into two orders of nobility, and the samurai forbidden to wear their swords. When this provoked an uprising among the former warrior nobles, they were put down by the newly established national conscript army and national police force. Slavery was abolished in 1873 and, in that same year, the government promulgated a new legal code which, in theory at least, declared all Japanese equal before the law. A system of public education was created by a decree which warned, "There shall be no community with an illiterate family, nor any family with an illiterate member." A university system was devised and thousands of Japanese were dispatched abroad to study Western ways.

All of this was accomplished by an Imperial Court government with ministers responsible only to the Mikado himself heading the various departments and the burgeoning bureaucracy. But the ferment of new ideas, the liberation of long-pent national energies, provoked a growing agitation for a more efficient, more democratic regime. This resulted in the promulgation, on February 11, 1889, of the so-called Meiji Constitution, a *gift* from the Emperor to his subjects. By its terms a *Diet* (parliament) was created which consisted of two houses: the House of Peers, populated by aristocrats, and the House of Representatives, whose members were to be elected by limited national suffrage. Neither house had much real power. Sole sovereignty in Japan continued to reside with the Mikado. He held supreme command over the government administration, over the armed forces, and through his veto over the Diet too.

During the last years of the nineteenth century Japanese industrialization made fantastically rapid strides. Telegraph, railroads, shipbuilding, cloth mills, iron foundries, arsenals, and factories of all kinds mushroomed over the landscape. Although owned and managed by private interests, Japan's industrialization was guided, fostered, often financed and guarded by the government. Despite the unavoidable growing pains of modernization (especially the uprooting of millions of peasants into the new factories and expanding cities, and the consequent grievances of a fast-growing new class of industrial workers), it could be fairly stated that by 1894 Japan had accomplished a miracle. In the space of two decades it had transformed itself from a feudal, agrarian society into a modern industrial nation. On the surface, anyway.

But what had really happened during this remarkable era? The Japanese ruling class, faced with the problem of defending their country from foreign domination and, at the same time, preserving their own power in a modern, industrialized society, had arrived at the solution of setting up a thinly disguised totalitarian state. For who were the Mikado's ministers and top bureaucrats except the reclassified daimyo? Who sat in the House of Peers except those same men? Who owned and managed Japan's new industries but those very same lords who had exchanged agrarian for industrial feudalism? Nor was Japanese society deeply transformed in its ideals and goals. The Emperor remained divine; his worship, enshrined in the Shinto religion, was official orthodoxy. The new public schools instilled in their pupils the old samurai virtues of blind obedience, endless endurance, and military discipline. Japan adopted the form, but not the content, of Western civilization. Her ruling classes wielded their new weapons—industry and nationalism—as once they had wielded their two-handed swords to preserve their personal interests. The martial spirit which had ruled Japan for a thousand years had not died; it now prepared to turn outward.

The first Japanese target was Korea. This "Hermit Kingdom," owing vague allegiance to the decayed Chinese Empire—it was policed by Chinese troops— was so weak, backward, and weakly governed that it made a tempting prize. If Japan did not seize it, Russia probably would—and that was unacceptable. "Korea is a dagger pointed at the heart of Japan!" cried the militarists. As early as 1876 the Japanese had "opened" Korea to the world in exactly the same way as Americans had opened Japan. Thereafter Japanese merchants flooded the country, soon dominated the Korean economy, and by 1893 had even cornered the national rice supply. Korean outrage at both Chinese taxation and Japanese exploitation led to endless uprisings and finally, in 1894, to a full-scale rebellion. Taking a leaf from the Western manual of imperialism, the Japanese promptly dispatched troops to Korea to "preserve order." But the worried Chinese, assuring Japan that they were perfectly able to police their subject state, also hurried troops into that unhappy land. After a few clashes, Japan declared war upon the Chinese Empire on August 1, 1894.

The Sino-Japanese War of 1894–1895 was a Japanese walkover. The new Imperial Navy, with iron-clad ships built in England and officers and crews trained in the English tradition, easily sank the Chinese fleet in the Battle of the Yellow Sea on September 17, 1894. Subsequently the Japanese Army, equipped with modern weapons and trained in the Prussian tradition, drove the Chinese from Korea, captured the Liaotung Peninsula with its fortress city of Port Arthur, seized the Shantung Peninsula, invaded Manchuria, and by February 1895 were threatening Peking itself. By the peace treaty of Shimonoseki concluded in April 1895, China recognized Korean independence and ceded to Japan the Liaotung Peninsula, the huge island of Formosa, and the Pescadore Islands. Japanese merchants were granted wide concessions in northern China and Japanese warships even allowed to patrol China's Yangtze River.

The swift Japanese victory startled the European powers. Here was a new, modern, aggressive *Asiatic* state jostling for a place at the imperialist table where Western nations feasted on the carcass of the hapless Chinese Empire. It was not to be borne! Russia, supported by France and Germany, demanded that Japan return the Liaotung Peninsula to China. The Meiji ministers saw no alternative but to accede.

Japanese public opinion, outraged by this European interference, enthusiastically supported a government program of tremendous military and naval expansion—even though this would consume more than 53 percent of the national budget. Japanese feelings were further embittered when, in 1898, the Russians themselves secured a leasehold on the Liaotung Peninsula from China while Germany gobbled up Shantung.

That same year a new and improbable imperialist power made its appearance in the Far East: The United States, as part of the spoils of its "splendid little war" against Spain, secured the huge Philippine Archipelago and several other Spanish trans-Pacific islands. While the hapless President William McKinley "prayed for Divine Guidance," the same wave of American jingoism engulfed Hawaii, where thousands of emigrant Japanese resided, and floated a new United States Navy even more threatening than Commodore Perry's "black ships." Furthermore the Americans, with their own expanding commercial interests in China, did not look with favor upon Japan's expansion on the Asiatic mainland.

Of course, as is apparent, the central fact of Far Eastern history from 1800 to 1949 was the weakness of the region's largest and potentially most powerful nation, China. It was into that huge vacuum of power that the European nations, the United States, and Japan were sucked in the quest for trade, influence, and strategic position. When and if that vacuum should be filled, the "Great Game" of imperialism in the Orient would come to a sudden end. Meantime the predator nations, including Japan, would jockey for position there and, at the same time, do everything they could to keep the Chinese sleeping giant weak.

American policy toward China was slightly more complex than that of her rivals. This was because American public opinion had "adopted" China as its favorite world orphan. Not only American merchants, but also thousands of American missionaries, teachers, and doctors had made their way into the Celestial Empire to further the great works of civilizing and Chris-

tianizing its bright, docile, apt, and cute inhabitants.
A commanding body of American voters thus demanded that their government, while enlarging United
States trade with China, at the same time "protect"
her from the rapacious schemes of less trustworthy
nations. It was to satisfy these twin demands that President Theodore Roosevelt, who had succeeded Mc-
Kinley upon his assassination in 1900, directed his
Secretary of State, John Hay, to propose to the European powers and Japan that they join the United States
in agreeing to pursue an "Open Door" policy in China.
None of the imperialist nations ought to so gorge themselves with territory or "influence" there as to damange
the commerce of any other. At one stroke Hay advanced
an idea which would protect American trade and yet
appear to the American public as a noble effort to preserve Chinese integrity. Perceiving nothing very
threatening to their real interests in this idealistic
commitment, the Europeans and Japanese were willing to humor the Americans and accepted their proposal. A happy confirmation of this new "cooperative"
attitude among the imperialist nations came during
the Boxer Rebellion of 1901. This hysterical attempt
on the part of the Chinese people (secretly supported
by the Empress Dowager) to rid their country of the
"foreign devils" was put down by an allied force of British, French, German, Russian, American, and Japanese troops, all cooperating handsomely in the slaughter of Chinese.

But upon reflection, even Theodore Roosevelt was
not entirely happy with the Open Door policy. For, as
he began to realize after 1901, America could have no
policy at all in the Far East unless she was willing to
back that policy by force in a showdown. But the
American people would never support a war for such

remote interests. They were already badly divided by the savage, endless campaign to subdue the Filipino independence movement. Although they had manfully taken up the "White Man's Burden" in those islands, they would spare neither the taxes nor the blood for any further Asiatic adventures. Indeed, Roosevelt observed, the Philippines had already become the "Achilles heel of our policy" in the Far East. Too far from home to be readily defensible, the new American colony was a hostage to peace in the Pacific. As early as 1902, American military men began to wonder how they could hope to protect the Philippines in the case of war with, say, Japan. Fortunately, for the moment, the Japanese were fully occupied elsewhere.

Elsewhere was Manchuria and Korea. The new Russian Tsar, Nicholas II, had concluded a treaty with the Chinese Empress Dowager which gave the Russians the right to construct a railroad through Manchuria. The Russians were busily taking advantage of this to move not only construction teams into the area, but also large military forces to "protect" their project. And in Korea the Russians were openly inciting violent Korean opposition to Japanese commerce. That Russia intended eventually to annex both Manchuria and Korea could not be doubted.

To counterbalance Russian power, the Japanese concluded an Alliance with Great Britain in 1902 whereby the English promised to come to Japan's aid in the event that while at war with one power (meaning Russia) she should be attacked by a third party (meaning Germany or France). Since the Royal Navy dominated the seas of the world, this left Russia without allies in the Far East.

For two years the Japanese attempted to negotiate their differences with the Tsar's government. But it was quite obvious that Nicholas had no intention of recognizing the "pretensions" of a people he referred to as "those little yellow savages." Accordingly, on February 9, 1904, the Japanese Imperial Fleet, under the command of Admiral Heihachiro Togo, steamed into the Russian naval base at Port Arthur and, by surprise torpedo attack, effectively crippled Russia's Far Eastern squadron—one day *before* Japan's declaration of war.

With command of the seas thus assured, Japanese armies were landed in Korea and Manchuria. Soon they had driven the poorly led Russians back to Mukden in Manchuria and Port Arthur on the Liaotung Peninsula. To reestablish Russian naval power in the Orient, Tsar Nicholas now dispatched the curious collection of naval antiquities which he called his Baltic Fleet halfway around the world from St. Petersburg to the China Seas. When, after an incredible ten-thousand-mile journey, the Russians arrived at the Straits of Tsushima on May 27, 1905, they were caught and totally destroyed by Admiral Togo's squadrons. Just a few weeks earlier both Mukden and Port Arthur had fallen to Japanese armies.

The Tsar, facing mounting unrest at home, and the Meiji government, whose financial resources were nearly exhausted, were both willing to make peace. Accordingly, both sides accepted the invitation of President Theodore Roosevelt to send representatives to Portsmouth, Maine, for a peace conference over which the American President would preside. On September 5, 1905, the Treaty of Portsmouth was agreed upon. By its terms Russia recognized Japan's paramount interest in Korea, agreed to withdraw her military forces from Manchuria, turning over to Japan her rail and mining interests there, and ceded to Japan her lease-

hold on the Liaotung Peninsula as well as the southern
half of Sakhalin Island. No *Russian* territory was
turned over (only Chinese) and no reparations were to
be paid.

When the Japanese public learned the terms of the
Treaty of Portsmouth they were outraged. Was it for
this they had submitted to huge taxes and suffered
more than 220,000 casualties? Antigovernment rioting
broke out in Tokyo and, because President Roosevelt
was seen as the villain in the peace, anti-American
sentiment flared. But the Meiji government quickly
subdued unrest (two thousand rioters were arrested in
Tokyo) and moved to consolidate the fruits of victory.
Japanese forces now took over the Liaotung Peninsula
and replaced the Russians in Manchura. As for Korea,
this turned into a Japanese "protectorate" and then
into an outright colony.

Americans, who had once regarded the Japanese
with the same kind of patronizing favor as they did the
Chinese, were alarmed by the speedy and decisive Japanese victory over Russia. Furthermore, although they
might look with bemused fondness upon Oriental cul-
tures overseas, they wanted none of that nonsense in
the United States. Native American racism, well prac-
ticed in dealing with blacks, Indians, and Mexicans,
had already been turned against Asiatics. The Pacific
coast states, especially California, passed laws forbid-
ding Japanese to own land or even to lease it. Hysteria
over Japanese immigration continued to mount despite
the fact that only some seventy-two thousand Japanese
arrived in the country from 1902 to 1907—years during
which millions of Europeans entered. And although
there were but ninety-three Japanese youngsters en-
rolled in San Francisco's public-school system, in 1906
the authorities there issued an edict expelling them in

order "to save White children from being affected by association with pupils of the Mongolian race." Worse than that, the west coast Asiatic Exclusion League persuaded Congress to pass new immigration laws which excluded Asiatics entirely. And, in 1907, a wave of anti-Japanese rioting broke out in San Francisco.

The Japanese, proud of their emergence as a modern nation, still riding the wave of nationalist fervor aroused by their victory over Russia and still, be it remembered, a people imbued with that fanatical samurai pride which itself amounted to racism, deeply resented all this. They also resented constant American admonitions to maintain the Open Door policy in China and to restrict their economic penetration of Manchuria. Surveying the Asiatic scene in 1907, the Japanese government realized that only the United States, among the Great Powers, could pose any real threat to their domination of the Orient. "In 1907," Admiral Fukudome later admitted, "the Imperial Navy made the United States its sole strategic enemy." For a few months it even appeared that jingoists on both sides of the Pacific might foment a war.

The crisis was averted by Theodore Roosevelt. He concluded an unofficial "Gentlemen's Agreement" with the Meiji government in 1908 whereby Japan agreed to herself limit the flow of Japanese emigrants to the United States—in return for the President's veto of the new immigration laws. That same year Uncle Teddy, brandishing his "Big Stick," dispatched the sixteen battleships of the "Great White Fleet" on a "goodwill tour" of the world—mainly as a warning to Japan. By the time the fleet reached Tokyo, Japanese feelings had been calmed and it received a royal welcome. Nonetheless, American naval expansion continued, work was pushed on the Panama Canal, and the United

States began construction of large naval bases at Cavite in the Philippines and Pearl Harbor in Hawaii.

But while the two Pacific rivals sought to maintain an uneasy status quo in the Far East, an event occurred which would one day shatter the balances of power there forever. In 1911 the long-suffering Chinese people, led by American-educated Dr. Sun Yat-sen, finally overthrew the detested Manchu Dynasty and proclaimed a Republic. The United States regarded this revolution with patronizing approval, the Japanese (who had harbored and financed some of the Chinese revolutionaries) with mixed feelings. To them anything that weakened the authority of the old Imperial central regime was welcome—for that facilitated further Japanese penetration. A Chinese Republic, on the other hand, with, if they read Sun Yat-sen's program aright, a xenophobic, strongly nationalistic bias might well establish a central government strong enough to resist Japanese encroachments. But the Meiji ministers needn't have worried. The Chinese warlord Yüan Shih-k'ai wrested control of the rebellion in north China from Sun and set himself up as head of the new government in Peking. Following his lead, other warlords fell upon the prostrate carcass of the fallen Empire and set up gangster-style fiefdoms everywhere. China was plunged into civil strife that would last for more than three decades.

In July 1912 the Mikado Meiji died—and with him much of the Imperial prestige that had shielded his ministers from popular pressures. Political leaders who had not been able to derive sufficient authority from the Emperor would have to derive some, at least, of that authority from the support of political parties. Such parties—a kaleidoscope of shifting names, purposes, and followings—had been gathering strength in

Japan ever since the turn of the century. Basically, except for the small, vociferous, and savagely repressed socialists, they represented a radical and a conservative approach to national problems. Foreign observers, especially Americans, were often misled into distinguishing liberal and reactionary groups among them—but their goals were the same.

Both radicals and conservatives agreed that Japan's rapidly expanding population required what the Germans called *Lebensraum*—living space, extensive new national territories. They also agreed that this burgeoning population could not be fed by the relatively scanty domestic food production—food would have to be imported. This in turn demanded that Japan's large new industries must have secure foreign markets and sources of raw materials. It was a case of export or starve. They also agreed that Japan, as the leading Asiatic power, owed it to her neighbors to take them under her wing for their own protection and "enlightenment." Both sides looked forward to the creation of a "Greater East Asia Co-Prosperity Sphere" led and dominated by Japan. They differed not in aims, but in methods.

Conservative politicians held that Japan's goals could be achieved by economic penetration, emigration—there were already large and fast-growing Japanese communities throughout the Far East—and commercial expansion. Provided the Western powers, especially the United States, were not provoked, Japan ought to be able to achieve her goals through peaceful means. Radical politicians, on the other hand, argued that only the outright annexation of huge chunks of the mainland could permanently assure Japanese prosperity. As for war with the West, that could best be avoided by a combination of judicious diplomacy and a forthright display of military power. Both radicals and conservatives (but especially the former) included among their followers a "lunatic fringe" of fanatics quite prepared to use rioting, violence, and political assassination to win the argument. Such, for example, was the Black Dragon Society, a secret order founded in the 1890s to pursue the goal of Japanese hegemony by whatever means necessary. Among its members were not only spies, blackmailers, and gunmen, but also leading industrialists, bankers, and military men as well as politicians of every nominal persuasion. Looking with some disdain upon all politicians, but supporting whichever side, radical or conservative, seemed opportune, were the all-powerful, totally independent Imperial Army and Navy, very ready to take matters into their own hands whenever and wherever their martial "honor" might be threatened. When in 1914 the World War broke out, both radicals and conservatives agreed that, on balance, Japan's interests would be best served by entering the conflict on the side of the Allies.

Japanese forces promptly undertook the conquest of the German concessions in China, mostly centered in the Shantung Peninsula, and of the German mid-Pacific island groups. Then, taking advantage of Western preoccupation with the battle in Europe, Japan turned on one of the Allies—China. On January 15, 1915, Japan presented to the hapless Yüan Shih-k'ai regime in Peking (Yüan had proclaimed himself Emperor by then) a list of Twenty-One Demands. These embraced a program of concessions which, if accepted by China, would transform her into a vassal state of the Japanese Empire. Yüan tried to stall, hoping for American intervention. But the United States, though vocal in her disapproval of this Japanese imposition, was, as Theodore Roosevelt had foreseen, unprepared to do anything concrete about it. After the Twenty-One Demands had been somewhat watered down, Yüan was forced to accept them. This led directly to his overthrow by his outraged subjects—and from the resulting chaos Japan was able to salvage few of her new gains.

There followed, as we have seen, the American-Japanese intervention in Soviet Siberia, Japanese adherence to the League of Nations (despite the fact that its charter would contain no antiracist clause) and the Washington Conference of 1921 which confirmed Japan in most but not all of her wartime spoils.

It was not any change in overall goals or basic aims which persuaded Japanese leaders to accept the Western proposals in Washington—the withdrawal of Japanese forces from Siberia, the return of Shantung to China, the abrogation of the Anglo-Japanese Alliance, the acceptance of "permanent" naval inferiority to Britain and the United States—but a realistic assessment of the world situation.

Since Lenin's Bolshevik government had secured its rule in Russia, Japan would *have* to withdraw from Siberia unless it wanted a full-scale war with the Soviet Union. And although Shantung was returned to China, Japanese economic domination and military infiltration both there and in Manchuria remained secure. As for the termination of the alliance with England—since Japan's only real potential enemy in the Pacific was the United States, and since Great Britain would never conceivably go to war with her American cousins, that treaty was meaningless anyhow. The acceptance of naval inferiority to the United States and Britain in battleships, while humiliating, also held certain advantages. It meant that the huge and fearsome new American fleets would be largely scrapped; and since

Japanese warships, unlike the American ones, were never far from their numerous Far Eastern bases, Japan was more interested in expanding her cruiser squadrons—upon which no numerical limitation had been placed. Finally, in return for all these "concessions" Japan secured the Anglo-Saxons' promise not to fortify new Pacific bases—while her own fortification program in that ocean was ignored.

Even so, radical Japanese politicians and the military leaders might not have been satisfied with the Washington agreements had it not been for the fact that a postwar depression had sent the Japanese economy reeling. It was essential to cut back somewhat on military and naval expansion during this period. Nevertheless, all through the twenties successive Japanese governments, whether "radical" or "conservative," would continue to meddle in Chinese affairs, continue the economic and military infiltration of Manchuria, Inner Mongolia, and other mainland regions. Indeed, as the twenties drew to a close Manchuria looked riper and riper for outright annexation. As we have seen, the United States during this same period had retreated into a shell of prosperous indifference to events overseas.

But if the curtain of Act I of The Great Pacific Drama, which had been raised by Commodore Perry in 1853, may be said to have descended at the Washington Conference in 1921, by the end of the twenties the intermission was over; the curtain was about to rise on the bloody events of Act II.

*Innumerable signs point out Fascism
as the doctrine of our age.*

BENITO MUSSOLINI

*The man who is born to be a dictator is not compelled;
he wills... he drives himself forward.*

ADOLF HITLER

*For years we have poured pails of manure at
each other. That should not, however, stop us
from coming to an understanding.*

JOSEF STALIN

7

The Great Dictators

To those who did not witness the phenomenon, it seems incredible that for nearly a quarter of this century, millions of supposedly sane, civilized, educated Europeans should have entrusted their destinies and their very lives to obviously psychotic leaders who openly promised them war. So shocking is this single, central fact, and so horrendous were its consequences, that some later observers have gone so far as to ascribe it to a mass "death wish," a peculiar malignancy of the human spirit. That the three totalitarian movements we must now examine were malign no one would question; that their rise represents something permanent and evil in human nature itself is, at best, debatable. What is certain is that fascism, Nazism, and Stalinism, the three "isms" which wracked the world from the twenties to midcentury, grew from the physical and spiritual wreckage of the First World War—although their seeds had been planted even earlier.

Fascism and Nazism, despite the semiliterate "definitions" advanced by their propagandists, were not "philosophies"—they were not even coherent political/social/economic systems. They were movements founded not upon thought but upon the megalomania of a few leaders and the emotional hysteria of vast masses of followers. Stalinism, although laying claim to the heritage of Marxist philosophy, was in reality no more than the resurrection of a tyranny as old in Russia as the land itself. Totalitarianism in any guise always represents not the result but the defeat of human reason, the cowardly retreat of human beings from real problems in the real world; it is an atavistic flight from responsibility into a dream (or nightmare) world of paranoid fantasies.

The leaders of these movements, the Great Dictators whose slightest whims once made the world tremble, seem preposterous and more than slightly ridiculous today—Mussolini with his bemedaled chest, his boastfulness, his posturing swagger; Hitler, looking like an evil edition of Charlie Chaplin's Tramp, with his hypnotic stare, his hysterical threats (the poet e. e. cummings described these two, respectively, as "strutmince" and "stink-brag"); and Stalin, a more complex character than the other two, more familiar yet improbable enough with his ponderous black mustache, his cold smile, and his ploddingly repetitious speeches. Yet hundreds of millions of people followed them.

The first of the dictators to achieve absolute power

was Benito Mussolini. He was born in northern Italy in 1883, the son of a socialist village blacksmith (who named him after Benito Juárez, the leader of the Mexican revolution) and a schoolteacher mother. Mussolini was educated in a Catholic seminary during his early years—but was expelled when he stabbed a fellow pupil. He remained an anti-clericalist for the rest of his life. In 1901 he became an elementary-school teacher who therafter tried to pass as a "professor" among his friends. Professor Mussolini attempted unsuccessfully to play the violin, wrote simple-minded essays on German literature, and could not seem to control his pupils. As a self-proclaimed socialist opposed to war, he fled Italian universal military service in 1902 and found refuge with a forged passport in Switzerland. There, after failing at a number of jobs, he was arrested in July 1902 as a beggar on the streets of Lausanne. The socialist leader Angelica Balabanov, who knew Mussolini in those days, later described him as a dirty, unkempt vagrant who cheated his friends, posed as an "intellectual," and avoided any kind of work. His socialism, declared Balabanov, was no more than a pose; he was really motivated only by a tremendous greed for recognition and a burning desire to revenge himself upon a society which somehow failed to perceive his worth. He was a loud and violent talker, a man who urged others to violence—but was himself so timid that he feared to walk home alone at night.

Mussolini returned to Italy in 1904, having reversed his principles not for the last time so that he could now accept military training. He emerged from the army a year later to engage in what was to always remain his primary interest—journalism. He worked hard at the newspaper business and also as a local organizer for the Italian Socialist Party. He was jailed several times for his vocal opposition to Italian imperialism in Africa and became editor of the Socialist newspaper *Avanti* (Forward). By 1912 he had become one of the most famous of Italian socialists. But it was observed that he inclined more and more to the violent end of the socialist spectrum—the belief in revolution by a minority in order to establish a socialist dictatorship, a growing fondness for power-for-the-sake-of-power.

When Italy entered the World War on the Allied side in 1915, Mussolini, scenting opportunity, abruptly dumped his Socialist allegiance to become a fiery nationalist. He was rewarded by certain Italian industrialists for this betrayal by being given a newspaper of his own, *Il Popolo d'Italia*, The Italian People, to publish. He had to endure a brief period of military service, seeing almost no combat but attaining the rank of corporal before a slight wound (incurred during hand-grenade practice) won him a medical discharge in 1917. Later he liked to modestly recall how the mere rumor of his presence in the front lines was sufficient to provoke abject terror among enemy forces, sending entire Austrian armies into headlong flight. In actuality he passed almost the entire war comfortably ensconced in his offices at *Il Popolo d'Italia*, heroically urging others to feats of sacrificial bravery on behalf of Italy's "Imperial Destiny."

In March 1919 the noncombatant warrior organized a small group of ex-socialists and unemployed war veterans into something he called the *Fascio di Combattimento* or Union of Combat. With a program that was no more than a confused hodgepodge of socialist schemes and nationalist rhetoric, the Fascio made no headway at first in Italian political life.

That life had been, since Italy's unification during the 1860s, an often violent, always confusing running battle between antagonistic groups: between rich industrialists and hungry workers in the north; between wealthy landowners and impoverished peasants in the south; between the Catholic Church and the Italian government, which had stripped the Pope of his secular powers; even between rival Mafia gangs controlling huge areas of Sicily and Sardinia. Anarchism, socialism, clericalism, royalism, imperialism, and a host of other poorly understood but fervently espoused "isms" kept the poisonous stew of Italian politics boiling for decades. Trembling on the lip of this cauldron was a succession of Italian governments presided over by various nervous prime ministers and owing nominal allegiance to an even more nervous king, Vittorio Emanuel.

The Italian government of 1915 had entered the war in hopes that glory would unify the country, divert popular unrest, and win for Italy large chunks of the Austro-Hungarian Empire. The Italian people were promised that their sacrifices during the fighting would be rewarded later by annexations and reparations which would, somehow, solve all their problems. Italians fought bravely amid the snow and ice of their high Alpine frontiers where 650,000 were killed but, in 1917, suffered a disastrous defeat at Caporetto. Nonetheless, the Treaty of London, in which the Allies promised Italy rich rewards if she fought on their side, required only that she participate—not necessarily succeed. Italy had participated at fearful cost. But then, at the Paris Peace Conference, when Italian Prime Minister Vittorio Orlando put forward Italy's claims, he found that largely due to Wilson's opposition, Italy was not to receive all her spoils—namely the Dalmatian coast of present-day Yugoslavia and its important port city of Fiume. Italians were outraged and the Orlando government fell.

Enlisting Italian anger and frustration, the famous poet-adventurer Gabriele D'Annunzio, a fiery, nationalistic egomaniac, organized a volunteer "army" of black-shirted war veterans, built around *squadristi*, squadrons of armed thugs not unlike the postwar German Freikorps and promptly seized the city of Fiume. The Italian government feared to interfere with this popular act of brigandage, but by 1921 Allied pressure and local Yugoslav resistance forced D'Annunzio's withdrawal. His brief year of glory had enlightened Mussolini.

During 1921 *Il Duce,* The Leader, as his followers now called Mussolini, began organizing his own squadristi, modeled on D'Annunzio's—even copying the latter's famous black shirts. Furthermore, Il Duce found a perfect target against which to rally support. The support came, initially, from unemployed war veterans, disillusioned socialists, and certain rich industrialists who saw in the Fascio a handy weapon against strikes and worker unrest. The target was Italy's nascent Communist movement—a group which, on the orders of the Third International, was now breaking away from the main Socialist Party. Fascist squadristi, on the pretext of combatting Communism, now launched a campaign of violence against trade unions, Left-wing newspapers, and socialist political gatherings. The Communists, organizing squadristi of their own, fought back—and blood flowed freely in Milan, Genoa, and other northern industrial cities. Observing all this, the wealthy landowners of southern Italy decided that the Fascist Party, as the Fascio di Combattimento was renamed in November 1921, was just what they needed to keep their impoverished, rebellious peasantry in line, and they too lent powerful support to Il Duce.

Having won the backing of the rich as their shield against the menace of Communism, Mussolini sought mass support by revising and rationalizing the Fascist program. He adopted, in shreds and fragments, the syndicalist theory of the Corporate State. First advanced in an encyclical by Pope Leo XIII in the 1880s, syndicalism was yet another theoretical attempt to reconcile some of the contradictions brought about by capitalist industrialization. In brief, it suggested that national life should be organized around work. That is, that each trade or occupation should be organized into a syndicate which would include workers, managers, and owners. Each such syndicate would, in turn, send elected representatives to a national parliament. Thus the economic interests of all would find political expression and the war of rich against poor be finally resolved. As amended by various later thinkers, syndicalism promised all things to all men. To the workers and peasants it promised representation in management, to industrialists and landowners it promised discipline among the workers and peasants, to all it promised an end to political strife. To Mussolini, who saw in it the perfect means of establishing a rigidly hierarchical society with the Fascist Party and himself on top, it was a useful political tool.

While anti-Fascist strikes, anti-Communist violence, and general social chaos spread throughout Italy, the Italian middle classes turned increasingly to fascism simply in the hope that it would restore law and order. Torn between the fear of Communism on the one hand and suspicions as to ultimate Fascist aims on the other, the great majority of basically nonpolitical, unorganized, moderate Italians opted for fascism as a lesser evil. Many were also swayed by Mussolini's fuzzy-headed, wildly romantic nationalism which emphasized the notion of a revitalized Italy embarking upon the "great adventure" of refounding the Roman Empire.

As Italian political life degenerated into extremist fanaticism and small-scale civil war waged by the Fascist squadristi against all opponents, succeeding Italian governments, of which there were no less than five between 1919 and 1922, found themselves increasingly unable to govern effectively. Membership in the Fascist Party grew enormously as Fascist candidates won seats in parliament and control of cities and towns in local municipal elections. By October 1922 Mussolini felt his hour had struck. Addressing a huge Fascist rally in Naples, Il Duce boasted: "Either the government will be given to us or we shall seize it by marching on Rome!"

The Italian government, headed by the essentially reasonable, weak-willed, moderate Premier Luigi Facta, decided to protect itself by calling out the Army. But when Facta presented the necessary decree of National Emergency to the king for his signature, Vittorio Emanuel, fearing for his throne and aware that the Army would probably join rather than suppress the Fascists, refused. When October 26, 1922 came, Fascist squadristi from all over the country were marching on Rome. Characteristically, after walking about two miles, Mussolini decided to take the train to the national capital. On October 30, the king invited him to form a new government according to parliamentary procedure—and from that moment parliamentary democracy was dead in Italy.

Within a very few months the Italian parliament, controlled by reactionary members and fearful of

Blackshirt violence, had voted Il Duce complete dic-
tatorial powers over every aspect of Italian life. During
the next few years the total "Fascistization" of the
country rapidly followed. Workers and peasants were
organized into syndicates totally controlled by Fascist
political bosses; the Italian armed forces and police
were purged of all who would not proclaim their blind
obedience to Il Duce; Italian schools and universities
were transformed into training camps for new Blackshirt legions; total censorship of the press, radio, and
publishing was imposed; a huge expansion of the armed
forces and a heavy program of military and naval rearmament brought profits to the rich, employment to
the masses, and some security to the middle classes;
all opponents of the new regime were exiled, imprisoned, or brutally murdered. Into the heads of all Italians (especially the young) was pounded the Fascist
doctrine: "Everything for the State, nothing outside
the State, nothing against the State." Within the span
of a single decade, from 1922 to 1932, Italian life was
totally reorganized into totalitarian forms. Italy's eventual destiny was openly proclaimed to be the conquest
of the entire Mediterranean region. Mussolini even
revived the Latin name for the Mediterranean—"Mare
Nostrum" (Our Sea) he called it as he strutted before
his legions of black-shirted fanatics. While vast crowds
chanted "Duce, Duce, Duce," he exhorted his people to
prepare for war. A nation must have, he proclaimed,
"a will to power," it must "learn to live dangerously."
While foreign observers, ignoring the brutality and
discounting the rhetoric, applauded the Fascists for
"making the trains run on time," the increasingly meg-
alomaniacal Duce forged Italy into his personal
weapon. The cowardly boaster who, as Angelica Balabanov had once observed, yearned to revenge himself

upon the world, was now prepared to do so on a vast scale. As a new decade opened Mussolini looked around to see where he could strike first.

An admiring observer of events in Italy (he copied some of Mussolini's methods) was Adolf Hitler, the German rabble-rouser we last observed writing his political testament in Munich's Landsberg Prison in 1923. Like Mussolini, Hitler was of humble, but not working-class, origins. He was born near Linz in Austria in 1889, the son of a minor customs official of the old Austro-Hungarian Empire. While Il Duce's father had been a socialist, Hitler's was an authoritarian who beat his son regularly—especially when the lad revealed his burning ambition to be an artist. In 1907 Hitler went to Vienna to make his career as an artist or architect—he wasn't too particular which—only to find his drawings rejected and the doors of the Academy closed to him. He warded off starvation by peddling small watercolors in Viennese cafés and, with little better to do, passed much of his time reading in the Vienna libraries. Not that he was, or ever had been, particularly studious; disciplined thought and learning both fatigued and bored him. But he idly skimmed some of the racist and totalitarian theories of nineteenth-century German philosophy. And it was during his years in this decaying capital of a decaying empire that Hitler absorbed the anti-Semitism that would become his consuming obsession. It was the Jews, Hitler discovered, who were responsible not only for all the world's woes, but also for his personal frustrations and sufferings. The streets of Vienna were, he later asserted, "the school of my life." Wallowing in frustrated rage and self-pity, the young Hitler yearned for some noble cause he could espouse.

He found it when Germany went to war in 1914. By

that time he had moved to Munich and was earning his living as a house painter. Discerning in the Kaiser the superman who embodied Germany's transcendental destiny of world conquest, Hitler enthusiastically enlisted in a Bavarian regiment. Like Mussolini, he eventually rose to the rank of corporal; but unlike Il Duce, he saw long, bloody periods of combat on the western front. Hitler was, by all accounts, a brave soldier; he was awarded the Iron Cross for personal valor. But his fighting days came to an end on October 14, 1918, when he was blinded by gas during a British attack. He was returned to Germany and, after two weeks of hospitalization, recovered his eyesight—only to lose it again when he learned, on November 9, that Germany was about to surrender.

Hitler's hysterical blindness soon passed—but not his burning sense of shame and indignation at Germany's defeat. It was impossible that a cause into which he had poured his soul, a cause for which he had personally suffered, could simply collapse. The German Army had been, he decided, infected and subverted by Communist agitators—how else explain the revolution which swept the Kaiser from power? Furthermore it had been betrayed by defeatists, war profiteers, and traitors on the home front. And who were all these evil people who had "stabbed Germany in the back"? They were, of course, the Jews!

Hitler's fierce hatred of Jews (deepened now into a burning psychosis), his detestation of republicans, Communists, liberals—of all who had "conspired" to shatter his wartime dreams—merging with an abnormal lust for personal power and domination, made him a formidable political fanatic. He was further helped by his powers of rhetoric. For it soon appeared that despite his harshly guttural Austrian accent, his speeches (into which he threw all the passionate hysteria of his soul) had the power to hypnotize as they inflamed German audiences. Soon he had attracted to his newly formed National Socialist German Workers' (Nazi) Party such footloose but fanatical followers as the crippled but clever ex-university instructor Joseph Paul Goebbels; the renowned German wartime flying ace Hermann Göring; the dull but laboriously dedicated ex-chicken farmer Heinrich Himmler; the savagely efficient Freikorps leader Ernst Röhm. It was with these men and hundreds of brown-shirted thugs organized into Röhm's *Sturmabteilung* (Storm Battalion; SA for short) that Hitler had attempted to seize power in Munich in 1923. That effort had, as we have seen, landed him in jail. When he emerged from Landsberg Prison in 1924, *Der Führer,* The Leader, as his followers now called him, decided that only through legal, constitutional means could he achieve supreme power in Germany.

Of course one would have to stretch the meaning of the words legal and constitutional somewhat to accommodate Hitler's subsequent activities. These included the enlargement of the SA into a private army and the transformation of the Nazi Party into a kind of state-within-the-state, complete with various "ministries" and bureaucracies and symbols—such as the twisted cross, the swastika. Many thousands of Germans found in the renovated Nazi Party after 1924 an outlet for their discontents, a fierce companionship that dispelled loneliness, rituals that boosted their egos, and above all a descipline which relieved them of all responsibility for their own lives.

But Hitler's political fortunes from 1924 to 1930 depended largely upon events beyond his control. There were some 30 million voters in the Weimar Republic and, at first, relatively few of them supported the Nazis. In the elections of 1925, which elevated the aged war hero Field Marshal von Hindenburg to the presidency, about 12 million Germans voted with the parties of the Left, the Communists, Socialists, and Social-Democrats, while 13 million cast their ballots with parties of the Right, ranging from Christian Democrats to Monarchists. At that time the Nazi Party numbered fewer than fifty thousand adherents. Most Germans, in supporting middle-of-the-road governments, were willing, it appeared, to give the Weimar Republic a chance. But that all depended.

It depended primarily upon the Republic's ability to assure economic stability and prosperity and to win Allied concessions upon the terms of the hated Versailles Treaty. The catastrophic German inflation of 1922–1923 had all but wiped out the German middle classes upon whose solid shoulders any democratic system would have to depend, and Germans were increasingly turning to radical movements for relief. The Dawes Plan of 1924, by alleviating the reparations burden and circulating American loans, brought new stability to German currency, which was now reissued at the rate of one *trillion* old marks for a single new mark. It also resulted in the French evacuation of the Ruhr. Furthermore, the liberal and intelligent Foreign Minister, Gustav Stresemann, who came into office in 1923 and guided German foreign affairs until his death in 1929, won German admittance to the League of Nations in 1926. Accepted once again into the family of nations, and enjoying relative prosperity, the German people during the late twenties seemed content enough with their experiment in democracy.

But appearances were deceiving; for all during this period the two extremist German political parties, the

Communists and the Nazis, increased their followings, slowly but surely. By 1929 each counted nearly two million registered members. Then, in the fall of 1929, prices on the American Stock Exchange took a sudden, disastrous plunge. As Wall Street went into a tailspin, the all-important American bank loans which had been floating the German economy began to dry up. As they did, German industry began to close down, unemployment rose, and prosperity vanished. Within a year Germany, like the rest of the industrial world, was plunged into the agony of the Great Depression. Unemployed workers, ruined small businessmen, frightened white-collar employees, the vast civil-service bureaucracy, impoverished farmers, turned en masse to the two radical parties, the Communists and the Nazis, whose orators promised simple, total solutions to complex problems. Once again Germany was plunged into political chaos as rival gangs, bands, and even battalions of armed Communist and Nazi thugs battled on the streets of German cities. All of which the German people blamed on the hapless Weimar Republic. In the elections of 1930, with 4 million now unemployed, the Nazis increased their seats in the Reichstag from 12 to 107—thereby becoming the second largest party in the land after the Social-Democrats. In 1932, with 6 million unemployed, Hitler ran against Hindenburg for the presidency. Out of some 36 million votes cast in a runoff election, the eighty-five-year-old Field Marshal won a majority of 1,100,000 against Hitler and the Communist candidate Ernst Thälmann—but it was apparent that Hitler, who now demanded that he be named Chancellor, could not be held off much longer.

There was one way the Nazis might have been defeated. This was by an alliance between the Communists and the Social-Democrats. Between them they controlled more than 200 seats in the Reichstag as against the Nazis' 107—and any Chancellor had to command a majority in that body. But despite the appeals of the Social-Democrats, the Communists refused to cooperate, for reasons we shall examine shortly. In the upshot, after various political maneuverings, Hindenburg had no recourse but to name Hitler Chancellor on January 30, 1933. On that night the Führer watched as thousands of his jackbooted storm troopers marched through the streets of Berlin, drums booming, flaming torches held aloft, voices raised in hoarse rendition of old German battle hymns. Like Mussolini ten years earlier, Hitler now had an entire powerful nation at his disposal—a nation he too would forge into a mighty weapon with which to fulfill his paranoid fantasies.

With a teutonic thoroughness and efficiency which made Il Duce's fascism seem indecisive by comparison, Hitler "Nazified" Germany. He had long since gained the financial backing of the rich by promising to smash the Communists—now he secured the support of the powerful German General Staff by promising the creation of a mighty war machine. The last vestiges of German democracy were drowned in the roars of *Sieg Heil!* (Hail Victory!) with which the Nazi-packed Reichstag proclaimed Hitler Führer of the entire nation. All other political parties were disbanded, trade unions were smashed, the schools and universities were taken over by Nazi party members, the press, radio, and motion-picture industry were converted into government propaganda organs, Nazism and worship of the Führer were elevated to a state religion, a harsh and pitiless persecution of German Jews was begun. All who opposed this program in any way were quickly murdered or sent by the hundreds of thousands to the slow death of barbarous concentration camps. As the German people stolidly proclaimed their allegiance to *Ein Volk, Ein Reich, Ein Führer* (One People, One Realm, One Führer), Hitler boasted that his Third Reich (the first had been Charlemagne's, the second the Kaiser's) would "last for one thousand years!"

As to the Führer's international objectives, these had been frankly disclosed in his book, *Mein Kampf.* First he would free Germany from the shackles of Versailles; Germany would openly rearm on a vast scale and German troops would reoccupy and fortify the demilitarized Rhineland. Then Germany would turn to the task of absorbing all Germans who lived beyond her borders. This meant *Anschluss* or annexation with Austria, expressly forbidden by the Treaty of Versailles, the repossession of the now Czechoslovak Sudetenland, and the wresting from Poland of Upper Silesia, Danzig, the Polish Corridor, and all those German territories awarded her at Versailles. All of this accomplished, Germany would be prepared to resume the *Drang nach Osten* (drive to the east) interrupted in 1918. For the Germans, the world's Master Race, needed *Lebensraum* (living space). She would carve it out of Poland, Russia, and the Ukraine. All of eastern Europe would be repopulated with German settlers and become a vast reservoir of food, raw materials, and slave labor. As for the peoples presently inhabiting these regions, they, like the Jews, were of clearly "inferior races"—those who were not enslaved would be simply exterminated. If the Western Allied powers attempted to interfere with this program of conquest—in view of their fear of Communism, Hitler was confident they would not—then they too would be smashed. Few foreigners bothered to struggle through the inane philosophy, preposterous megalomania, and turgid prose of *Mein Kampf*—and those who did simply laughed.

In view of the Führer's openly avowed aim of eastern conquest, it is ironical that the man who, as much as any other single individual, smoothed Hitler's rise to power in 1932 was the dictator of Hitler's ultimate Russian target—Josef Stalin. When, in those last days of the Weimar Republic, German Socialists and Social-Democrats begged Ernst Thälmann's Communists to join them in stopping the Nazis, the Communists had refused on Stalin's orders. "The path to a Communist Germany," Stalin insisted, "lies through Hitler." By which the German Communists assumed Stalin meant that the Nazis would soon make so terrible a botch of their regime that a Communist revolution would ensue. The Communist slogan was "The worse it gets, the better for us." But although Stalin probably believed this, his motives were darker and more devious than the German comrades imagined.

His motives had always been dark and devious, for the very simple reason that he was possessed of a profound and growing paranoia. Born in Russian Georgia in 1879 into a peasant family, Josef Dzhugashvili had been educated in a Russian Orthodox seminary in Tiflis. Expelled from school for having joined a secret Marxist study group, he drifted into revolutionary and criminal circles. For several years he combined his interests and his abilities by taking part in various bank robberies, holdups, and burglaries, the proceeds of which went to support Lenin's Bolshevik faction. At the same time, it appears that Stalin ("Steel," the underground pseudonym he adopted) acted as a part-time paid police spy, regularly betraying his Bolshevik comrades. By 1912, however, he dropped his police connections and dedicated himself wholly to Bolshevik aims.

Not that he ever seems to have clearly understood or much cared what those aims were. Lenin, Trotsky, and many of the other revolutionaries were, first and foremost, intellectuals—brilliant, cosmopolitan theorists; Stalin was a practical careerist, a dedicated bureaucrat. Unlike the Bolshevik leaders, Stalin was ill educated, spoke no foreign languages (not even Russian very well), and had no personal experience of the world outside Russia. He was not at home in the eloquent world of international socialism which, before 1917, was dominated by German, French, and Polish idealists. And he was very keenly, bitterly, fearfully aware of his provincialism, his intellectual failings, his lack of oratorical skills, of "charisma."

But what Stalin lacked by way of mental sophistication he made up for by a shrewd, opportunistic cunning and a ruthless determination natural to his violent background. Dominated by personal vanity and a lust for power, he was a man of great patience, a master of intrigue, and a political actor of genius. His gifts were not those of a Marxist revolutionary but rather those of a latter-day Genghis Khan.

During the two revolutions of 1917 Stalin played an insignificant part. N. N. Sukhanov, the diarist of the revolution, remembered him as a sort of "gray blur." After the first, the March Revolution, Stalin returned from exile in Siberia (where he had been since 1913) to St. Petersburg and was assigned to the staff of the Bolshevik newspaper, *Pravda* (Truth). In its pages, throughout the violent summer of 1917 and right up to October, Stalin's was usually a voice of conservative caution. For this he was more than once denounced by Lenin and ridiculed by Trotsky. After the Bolshevik seizure of power, Stalin was given the relatively unimportant post of Commissar for Nationalities on the theory that being of minority (Georgian) extraction himself, he would be able to deal with the problems of Russia's multifarious national groups.

Every revolution, once successful, attracts to itself political opportunists: fair-weather friends who join after the struggle only to advance their personal careers. The Russian revolution was no exception to this rule, and it was from among these dubious new recruits that the Commissar for Nationalities carefully constructed a personal following of political henchmen, well-placed bureaucrats who owed their positions to Stalin personally. He worked slowly, cautiously, advancing his interests surreptitiously until, when Lenin died in 1924, Stalin had the backing within the party to emerge as a serious candidate for its leadership. His appointment as Communist Party Secretary gave him opportunities to enhance his influence even further. His great rival, Trotsky (Lenin's obvious heir), had neglected to build himself a secure power base among the bureaucrats and, in 1926, paid the price for this omission when he was driven into exile. Shortly thereafter, having murdered all other pretenders, Stalin emerged as absolute master of the Soviet state.

But it must be recalled that Stalin did not invent the Communist dictatorship in Russia; that had been done by Lenin and Trotsky and the "idealistic" theoreticians. It was they who decreed the total domination of every aspect of Russian society by the Communist Party, they who devised a new and dreaded secret police, the *Cheka,* to enforce their will, they who nationalized all Russian commerce and industry, they who abolished all opposing political groups. Unlike Hitler and Mussolini, Stalin did not impose a dictatorship— he inherited one.

To keep that dictatorship secure from every threat was always Stalin's first and overriding concern. To do this he had first of all to defend the Soviet Union itself against the machinations of capitalists—and in pursuing this goal he followed a schizophrenic policy. On the one hand he employed the Third International to keep capitalist nations and their colonies in as much uproar as possible; on the other he actively sought friendly relations with those same capitalist governments on the official level. Announcing that, for the moment, the Soviet Union would eschew the goal of world revolution (while urging foreign Communist parties to continue to pursue it), Stalin declared that Russian energies must be devoted to "building socialism" at home. This was translated into a drive to industrialize at all costs, to solve food shortages by the enforced collectivization of the land, and to build up the power of the secret police and the Red Army. These goals, pursued through a series of "Five-Year Plans," were to succeed at the fearful cost of millions of Russian lives.

But it was not from the capitalist world alone, or even primarily, that Stalin most feared attack; rather it was from potential discontent at home, and *Communist* criticism from abroad. For Stalin never ever forgot how a mere handful of Bolshevik theoreticians, intellectuals wielding the moral outrage of the oppressed masses, had overthrown a previous Russian tyranny. He was able to murder or otherwise suppress—the Arctic slave-labor camps were filling rapidly—his domestic enemies, but he lived in constant dread of the emergence of a powerful, independent Communist voice from abroad which might rally Russian opinion to overthrow his regime. For this reason, while he manipulated foreign Communist parties to weaken capitalist governments, Stalin had no desire at all to see one of those parties actually achieve state power. For that would create an alternative Communist base of operations which would be difficult, if not impossible, to control.

And this, in turn, went far to explain Stalin's instructions to the German Communist party in 1932. After having opposed and assailed the Weimar Republic during its entire history, German Communists had helped mightily to bring it to the brink of catastrophe. When it fell, Germany might go Communist or Nazi. Stalin, for the reasons outlined above, preferred the Nazi alternative. His orders to the German Communist Party in 1932 amounted to a demand that they commit political and personal suicide. They obeyed and Hitler triumphed. Of course Stalin, like most other foreign observers, perceived no real threat from the new German Führer—he was a semicomic aberration who would soon pass.

And so, from the wreckage and despair of the World War, the Great Dictators fashioned their totalitarian regimes. For despite the deeper historical roots of revolutionary discipline in Russia, authoritarian racism in Germany, and nationalist swagger in Italy, it must not be forgotten that it was the great carnage, the mortal and moral catastrophe of 1914–1918, which so crippled European society as to make these new tyrannies possible. The First, not the Second World War, was *the* disaster of our century; from it flowed ills with which we still grapple. As for those nations stricken most brutally by that disaster, their peoples embraced the vicious "isms" we have described with a kind of defiant glee. Totalitarianism was, they assured the rest of mankind, the irresistible "wave of the future."

*In all the years of my husband's public life
I never once heard him make a remark which
indicated that any crisis could not be solved.*

ELEANOR ROOSEVELT

8

The Crisis of Democracy

Tyranny the wave of the future? It seemed so not only
to Nazis, Fascists, and Stalinists, but also to many citizens of the Atlantic democracies. As the decade of the
thirties began, standing amid the wreckage of national
economies shattered by the Great Depression, many
Britons, Frenchmen, and Americans began to fear that
the deepest problems and contradictions of modern industrial society could never be solved by democratic
methods. What did the political forms of freedom matter to people without shelter, without enough to eat,
without hope for the future? What good was personal
liberty to tens of millions of people who had no jobs nor

any real prospects of work? Even so stout a champion
of freedom as Winston Churchill, now a Conservative
Member of Parliament, expressed his fears. Surveying
the bleak horizon in 1930, he wrote: "This problem of
unemployment is the most torturing that can be presented to a civilized society.... One may even be par-
doned for doubting whether institutions based on adult
suffrage could possibly arrive at the right decisions
upon the intricate propositions of modern business and
finance.... You cannot cure cancer by a majority vote.
What is wanted is a remedy."

The disease itself was not new—depressions in the
industrialized nations had been a recurring phenom-
ena since the advent of capitalist economies. They
seemed to come in cycles and were, claimed economists,
inevitable and even necessary. But that economic collapse which would be known to history as the Great
Depression was of a depth and magnitude so surpassing
all others that it seemed to presage the downfall of
civilization itself. It came to many industrial nations
almost simultaneously; its causes and course varied
slightly from land to land. But most *probably* it was
triggered by financial collapse in the United States—
and the American experience of it was fairly typical of
what happened elsewhere.

First of all, at the end of October 1929 (just a few
weeks after President Herbert Hoover proclaimed the
arrival of eternal prosperity) the Stock Market on Wall
Street collapsed. Prices of stocks tumbled disastrously
and kept on falling. As corporations, utilities, insurance companies, banks, and thousands of individuals
lost the huge amounts of money they had invested in
stocks, a chain reaction commenced. Insurance companies and banks started to fail and millions of people
lost their life's savings with them; corporations went

bankrupt or cut production to the bone in order to survive; unemployment mushroomed to tremendous proportions. All of which destroyed purchasing power so that more and more companies, unable to sell their products, retrenched or went out of business; this in turn increased unemployment still further. The chain reaction quickly led to a vicious, seemingly inescapable cycle of misery.

The causes of the Great Depression are still a matter of debate, but briefly ... The collapse of the Stock Market was *probably* brought about by wild speculation which, during the decade before 1929, had swollen stock prices way beyond their true values. When stock prices began to slip, loss of confidence led to panic selling, which snowballed into a landslide of catastrophe. Due to the lack of any governmental controls whatsoever, corporations, financial institutions, and banks had overinvested their own and other people's money so heavily that many were unable to absorb their losses. From that point, the chain reaction is fairly clear.

Why was recovery so difficult? For several *probable* reasons. First of all, the economy was lopsided. The large profits made by American industry during the twenties had not been properly distributed. Although worker productivity increased by 25 percent during that period, wages went up barely 8 percent. Business and industry were not sharing their profits with labor—instead they were investing too much of those profits in the already overblown Stock Market, skimming off too high a percentage in personal high-management incomes. Labor unions during this period were all but powerless; most American workers remained unorganized. The end result was that there was no reservoir of mass purchasing power or savings to keep the wheels of industry turning or to restart them once they'd stopped. Second, farm income during the twenties, as we have already noted, was always low—like industrial workers, farmers represented no potential purchasing power. Third, much too high a proportion of the national wealth, in the absence of government regulation, had simply been stolen by corrupt owners and managers of big business. This was especially true in the field of public utilities, where a system of so-called holding companies—a system so intricate that even its creators had difficulty explaining it to Congressional investigating committees—milked consumers unmercifully. Fourth, high tariff barriers erected in all countries at the behest of industrialists to protect native manufacturing against foreign competition had effectively crippled international trade. Fifth, there was simply not enough money in circulation. All currencies were based on gold at that time, and governments were reluctant to devalue their currencies for fear of inflation. And, finally, there was no government intervention in the economy. The aim of every Republican administration since Harding had been to save money, to balance the national budget. The idea that government itself might step in as a purchaser of last resort to bolster the economy was heresy and smacked of Godless Bolshevism.

As we have pointed out, these were the *probable* causes of the Great Depression—and there were others; all have been endlessly debated by historians in the years since 1930. What has never been debated was the absolute misery of the American people during that time. Misery—and frustration. Living in a land of plenty, with broad and fertile fields capable of growing food for most of the world, with abundant natural resources of every kind, with the mightiest industrial machine on earth, with a large, skilled, and hard-working population, the majority of Americans were reduced to impoverishment. While crops rotted in fields and warehouses, millions went hungry; while coal mines shut down and public power companies went bankrupt, millions shivered through heatless winters; while mills and factories closed, millions lacked everything that industry could provide.

Nor was there, in 1930, any "welfare cushion" to help abosrb the blow. Unlike Germany, France, and a few other more advanced nations, the United States enjoyed no social security system. Such things as unemployment insurance, food stamps, disability benefits, welfare payments—all were unknown. Nor were there, aside from a few craft unions of the American Federation of Labor, such things as union retirement funds. In those days the poor, the unemployed, had to rely on scanty state relief funds and private charity. As depression deepened, states lost more and more tax income, so that they were less and less able to help, while private charitable organizations were soon overwhelmed by the growing load of despairing clients. That the Federal government might have any responsibility to alleviate the distress of its citizens was looked upon as a thoroughly un-American idea. Government regulation, support, or intervention of any kind would be, warned the rich, the beginning of socialism, the utter destruction of the free-enterprise system—and besides, it would be bad for the character of the people to accept government aid; they would become lazy and indolent.

By 1932 there were no less than 11 million people unemployed—about 25 percent of the labor force. In the countryside hundreds of thousands of farmers were being dispossessed as banks and loan companies foreclosed mortgages on fields and homes. On city streets ragged lines of people stretched for many blocks outside soup kitchens. Thousands of unemployed men swallowed their pride and sold apples on street corners—a thinly disguised form of begging. Hundreds of thousands of homeless people built tarpaper and scrap-tin shanties in public parks, these huge settlements of despair being dubbed "Hoovervilles" by their bitter inhabitants. It was found that a growing number of children in the public schools could no longer do their studies properly—they were drowsy with undernourishment. The pressures of poverty broke up family life so that all across the country bands of homeless children roamed the land, seeking handouts from farmers who were themselves impoverished. Worst of all, a mighty wave of confused fear spread over the nation. Something, somewhere, was terribly wrong. The American dream had turned into a nightmare. The social-economic system that Americans had been taught to revere for more than a century had simply collapsed.

Out of poverty, despair, and fear grew anger. By 1932, with more than *13 million* now unemployed, people began taking matters into their own hands. In Detroit, Chicago, New York, and other cities large mobs looted food markets and department stores while frightened police looked on. In the countryside farmers organized vigilante committees which threatened to (and sometimes did) lynch mortgage foreclosers—and when local sheriffs tried to enforce the law they were often driven away by armed and ugly crowds. Amid the growing chaos new voices were heard—voices which called for revolution, voices which promised total solutions of either the Communist or Fascist variety.

The rich were frightened; many transferred their money abroad while some even fled the country. And the government of Herbert Hoover was frightened—when, in 1932, thousands of unemployed World War veterans, many with their wives and children, gathered in Washington as the "Bonus Army" to demand that Congress now pay them the war bonuses they'd been promised years before, the President ordered the Army, commanded by Chief of Staff General Douglas MacArthur and his aide, Major Dwight D. Eisenhower, to "liberate" the capital with bayonets and tear gas. The American people, it seemed, had become the enemy. As for Federal intervention to alleviate suffering or help the economy, Hoover was utterly opposed. Indeed, he stoutly refused to recognize the extremity of the crisis. "Prosperity," he assured visitors, "is just around the corner." Years later, summing up his views on a 30 percent unemployment rate, he wrote: "Many persons left their jobs for the more profitable one of selling apples." To a newsman in 1931 he confided, "Nobody is actually starving. The hoboes, for example, are better fed today than they have ever been. One hobo in New York got ten meals in one day." Government, he claimed, should exert all its efforts to balancing the budget. That would reassure business leaders, who would then reopen their plants, etc., etc. His was the ancient economic theory always and everywhere advanced by the wealthy—make the rich richer and some of the wealth will trickle down to the masses below.

There was one important, saving factor in an increasingly ugly situation; 1932 was a presidential election year. If a new government which would *do* something could be installed in Washington, then maybe the voices of revolution, of totalitarian solutions, would be stilled. The American people, with a patience and fortitude that amazed foreign observers, would give their free institutions a chance to solve their problems—perhaps a last chance.

The political leader to whom most Americans turned in 1932 was the Democratic presidential candidate, Franklin Delano Roosevelt—an improbable friend of "the common man." Improbable because FDR, as he was universally called, had been born in 1882 to a heritage of ease and wealth. His family roots went back to the earliest Dutch settlers of Nieuw Amsterdam—for centuries Roosevelts had been among the landed gentry whose large estates dominated New York's lower Hudson River valley. While not superrich like the Du Ponts, the Astors, or the Rockefellers, the Roosevelts were wealthy enough to live like country gentlemen. Most of them had looked with distaste upon the rough and energetic politics of cousin Theodore Roosevelt when he became President in 1900. Young Franklin Roosevelt was raised, if not in the lap of luxury, certainly in the lap of security and comfort. Indeed it was to be one of the bitterest reproaches hurled at him by the rich that he had "betrayed his class."

After several years of private tutoring, the young FDR was sent to a fashionable private school, Groton School, whose headmaster, the Reverend Endicott Peabody, instilled in his pupils a strict sense of *noblesse oblige*—of the obligations owed by the rich to their fellow men. Later FDR attended Harvard College and, finally, Columbia University's Law School. When he chose a bride in 1905, it was a girl not only of his own class, but from his own family—distant cousin Eleanor Roosevelt. After passing the New York State Bar examination in 1907, he joined a Manhattan law firm and soon found himself drawn into local politics. The fact that FDR became a Democrat rather than a Republican like all the other Roosevelts was primarily due to Democratic preponderance in New York City. In 1910, at the urging of Democratic politicians, FDR ran for the State Senate from his home district around the family estate at Hyde Park. Surprisingly, he won in a traditionally Republican area. His reformist activities in Albany attracted the attention of Woodrow Wilson who, in 1913, invited him to become Assistant Secretary of the Navy.

Roosevelt proved to be an energetic and highly capable administrator of naval affairs all through the World War. He tried to enlist for overseas combat, but was constrained to remain at his post in Washington. There he was a close observer and admirer of Woodrow Wilson's reform administration and a loyal supporter of the President's campaign to enlist the United States in the League of Nations. When, at the San Francisco convention in 1920, the New York delegation sullenly refused to join in a demonstration of approval for Wilson, FDR physically wrested the state standard from a pair of Tammany Hall politicians and joined the parade. From that convention, to his considerable surprise, FDR emerged as the vice-presidential candidate. Despite a gallant campaign 1920 was, as we have seen, a Republican year. When the votes were in, FDR retired to his New York law practice and, in August 1921, took his family for their annual vacation to Nova Scotia's Campobello Island. There he was suddenly stricken by poliomyelitis which left him paralyzed from the waist down. The doctors assured him that he was lucky to be alive at all, that he would never walk again, that he was a permanent invalid.

Roosevelt refused to accept this life sentence. As soon as he had recovered sufficiently to use a wheelchair he undertook a rigorous course of exercises designed to win back the use of his legs. Nor would he consider himself an invalid—he never permitted his crippled condition to darken his essential vigor or optimism. Dr. Ross McIntyre (later FDR's White House physician) said, "No one ever saw him indulge in so much as a moment of self-pity." In 1924, hearing about the supposedly therapeutic value of the hot natural springs at a ramshackle southern resort, FDR began frequenting Warm Springs, Georgia. He found that swimming in the buoyant waters of the Springs brought definite improvement to his paralyzed legs. Soon other paralytics, reading in the press about FDR "swimming himself back to health," began to join him. Eventually Roosevelt organized a Warm Springs Foundation, which became a national center for the treatment of polio victims. After FDR became President, the Foundation organized an annual "March of Dimes" campaign to raise funds—funds which, eight years after FDR's death, would enable Dr. Jonas Salk to conquer the disease which had never conquered the President. There can be little doubt that FDR's lonely battle against invalidism—by 1928 he was able to walk, with the aid of heavy steel leg braces and canes—brought iron into his soul and reinforced his optimistic faith that the human spirit could triumph over any obstacle. His personal courage would later inspire a nation that badly lacked courage to face its future.

Roosevelt refused to allow his condition to obstruct his politcal activities, although, during the early twenties, these were minimal. Through constant correspondence he maintained and even enlarged the circle of his political supporters. In this he was powerfully aided by his wife, who now became his mobile eyes, ears, and voice. Eleanor Roosevelt, reluctantly at first, then with growing enthusiasm and ability, became her husband's wide-traveling representative and reporter.

At the Democratic Convention of 1928, FDR, walking slowly, painfully, but under his own power to the lectern, made the principal nominating speech in support of Al Smith. In September he ran for Smith's former office, the governorship of New York. Smith lost to Hoover that year, but FDR won handsomely. When Republican newspapers questioned the new governor's ability to fill his office, Smith replied, "The Governor of New York State does not have to be an acrobat."

As New York's governor, Roosevelt, after the onset of depression in 1929, began to experiment with those programs of reform and relief which he would later exercise on a national scale. And he attracted to him many of the men whose "radical" views on combatting the disaster would become national policy: men like his State Relief Administrator, Harry Hopkins, as well as the "college boys," Rexford Tugwell, Adolf Berle, Raymond Moley, and Felix Frankfurter, who recruited the bright young men later called Roosevelt's "brain trust." By 1932 Roosevelt had become the obvious Democratic presidential candidate; his fight for the nomination was relatively painless. And, in that year, he easily defeated an embittered Herbert Hoover to become President of the United States.

Suddenly a brave new voice rang out, not only across America, but around the world. In his inaugural address in March 1933, from a capital guarded by bayonets and machine guns, FDR declared: "Let me assert my firm belief that the only thing we have to fear is fear itself.... This Nation asks for action, and action now.... The people of the United States have not failed." Thoughtful, deeply worried men in France, England, and other lands equally burdened by depression and social disintegration thought they saw, in distant Washington, a spark of hope. "Henceforth," proclaimed the French newspaper *Le Temps,* "democracy has its chief." The English economist John Maynard Keynes wrote to FDR a few months later: "You have made yourself the trustee for those in every country who seek to mend the evils of our condition by reasoned experiment within the framework of the existing social order."

The trustee set to work, during the spring of 1933, with an energy, vigor, and daring that left the nation breathless. During the first so-called Hundred Days after his inauguration, FDR's administration commenced a veritable peaceful revolution of American society—the New Deal. Soon that huge alphabet soup of Federal agencies and bureaus and commissions which were to permanently transform the nation's economic structure came into being. The Agricultural Adjustment Administration (AAA) brought relief to American farmers; the National Recovery Administration (NRA) attempted to reorganize and revitalize American industry; the Public Works Administration (PWA) and the Works Progress Administration (WPA) rebuilt the nation's public domain and gave employment to millions; the Securities and Exchange Commission (SEC) brought the Stock Exchange under control; the Civilian Conservation Corps (CCC) enlisted the nation's youth to preserve forests and national parks—these and dozens of other agencies were the New Deal's weapons to combat the crisis. Later came the Social Security Act, which finally provided a measure of security for the sick, disabled, unemployed, and elderly. And, with the passage of the Labor Relations Act in 1936, labor unions gained government support in their battle against big business. A new labor organization, the Congress of Industrial Organizations (CIO), came into being and waged a small-scale civil war across America's industrial landscape to organize millions of workers who'd been neglected by the more conservative American Federation of Labor (AFL).

Not all of these weapons were successful. Some, like the NRA, were declared unconstitutional by the Supreme Court; others were to prove simply ineffective. All were bitterly opposed by the rich. And although unemployment had been cut to 8 million by 1935, the depression continued. But that was not the vital point. The vital point was that the American people perceived that their free institutions could, after all, adapt themselves to combat economic and social inequalities and woes. It seemed, through the humane atmosphere of the New Deal, that "the forgotten man" had not been forgotten after all. People felt they had a friend in the White House who led a government which was, once again, theirs. They retained faith in democracy itself.

As for Roosevelt, he never questioned that faith. He obstinately refused to define or constrict his policies within any theoretical framework. He was completely pragmatic; if one measure did not work he would immediately adopt another, continuously experimenting without regard for theory until he succeeded. He remained firmly opposed to any kind of "total solutions" which might infringe upon personal liberties or limit the workings of free institutions. The "isms" so loudly touted overseas and, as the decade worn on, at home, were to him not only repugnant but also irrelevant to real problems in the real world. When asked once what his political philosophy was, FDR looked puzzled and annoyed. "Philosophy?" he replied. "Why, I'm a Christian and a Democrat—that's all." Yet he was well aware that the fight for democracy he was waging in America had wider implications overseas.

Roosevelt had come to power at the same time, and

upon the same flood of despair, which had raised Adolf Hitler to German's leadership. Many throughout the world compared their efforts and their solutions. But, admonished Winston Churchill, "To compare Roosevelt's efforts with those of Hitler is to insult, not Roosevelt, but civilization." After FDR's tremendous electoral victory in 1936 when he defeated the hapless Republican candiate Alfred M. Landon, carrying every state but Maine and Vermont, Churchill observed, "His impulse is one that makes toward the fuller life of the masses of the people in every land, and which, as it glows the brighter, may well eclipse both the lurid flames of German Nordic self-assertion and the baleful, unnatural lights which are diffused from Soviet Russia."

Certainly the European democracies stood in need of inspiration. England was hard hit by the Great Depression and so was France. In both countries millions were unemployed, industries were crippled, and business was at a standstill. Successive national governments in England, headed by Laborite Ramsay MacDonald (1931–1935), Conservative Stanley Baldwin (1935–1936), and Baldwin's successor, Neville Chamberlain, grappled with many of the same problems that beset the New Deal in America. These were complicated in Britain by the demands of empire, by an aging industrial plant, and by a still-flourishing class system which most Englishmen revered and yet resented. But by adopting policies which, in their humane concern for the people's welfare, reflected the spirit of FDR's programs, English politicians averted social catastrophe. And in Britain, as in America, it turned out that the traditions of liberty and self-government could, with a little help, weather the storm.

Like their American cousins, the British people remained firmly committed to democracy.

France had her own traditions of liberty and freedom—but these derived not, like the Anglo-Saxons', from the long, slow development of parliamentary forms, but rather from the traditions of the great French Revolution of 1789—and from the combats, uprisings, and revolutions which had inflamed French political life ever since. Under the pressures of the Great Depression, the institutions of the Third Republic trembled. In February 1934 royalists and socialists fought out their differences on the streets of Paris—and therafter the same kind of political guerrilla warfare which had wracked Germany began to gather momentum in France. With large and vigorous Socialist and Communist Parties facing a smaller but heavily financed coalition of Right-wing extremists and Fascists organized into the *Action Française,* liberal and moderate politicians found smaller and smaller ground for maneuver. After a kaleidoscope of governments followed each other in rapid confusion, an alliance of Socialists and Communists prevailed to bring to power the so-called Popular Front government of Premier Léon Blum. Himself a moderate socialist with liberal impulses, Blum embarked uoon a New Deal-type program of relief and reform. But French political life was too polarized to provide the long-term support he needed; in 1937 Blum was forced to resign. Succeeding governments remained weak while French confidence in France's democratic institutions steadily eroded.

Of course the Great Dictators of the world—Hitler, Mussolini, and Stalin—regarded the struggles and flounderings of democracy in Britain, France, and the

United States with amused contempt. While Stalin continued to attempt the subversion of free governments through his manipulation of the client Communist Parties of the Third International, Hitler and Mussolini were busily arming for a frontal assault upon freedom. In this they were mightly aided by the effects of the Great Depression abroad. For the peoples of the democracies were much too involved with their own struggles for survival to pay any attention to the sinister rumblings of distant totalitarian volcanoes.

Yet some democratic leaders—notably FDR in the United States and Winston Churchill in England—were watching the growth of tyrannical power in Germany, Italy, and Russia with mounting concern. Franklin Roosevelt may have had in mind this potential conflict looming on the horizon when he spoke to one hundred thousand cheering supporters in Franklin Field, Philadelphia, on June 27, 1936, to accept renomination for the presidency. He lifted American eyes beyond domestic troubles when he pointed out, "We are fighting to save a great and precious form of government for ourselves and for the world." Then, with a flash of prophetic insight such as Abraham Lincoln might have known, the President declared: "There is a mysterious cycle in human events. To some generations much is given. Of other generations much is expected. This generation of Americans has a rendezvous with destiny." What that destiny could entail, and what his own part in it would be, FDR made very clear. "I accept the commission you have tendered me," he said. "I join with you. I am enlisted for the duration of the war."

Who, thinking of the last ten years
Does not hear howling in his ears
The Asiatic cry of pain,
The shots of executing Spain,
See stumbling through his outraged mind
The Abyssinian, blistered, blind
The dazed uncomprehending stare
Of the Danubian despair . . .

W. H. AUDEN
New Year Letter, 1940

9

The Nightmare Decade

The events that punctuated the years 1930 to 1940 in Europe and Asia seemed, not only to an English poet but also to Americans who observed them from afar, a kind of Theater of Horror. It was as if you were chained to your seat and forced to watch the most hideously frightening film ever produced—unable to leave the theater, unable to avert your eyes from the bloody scenes enacted, ever more fearful that soon you would somehow be transformed from spectator to participant in the terrible drama. . . .

Here was a scene in which a Japanese Army ran amok through the ruins of the captured Chinese city of Nanking, raping, cruelly torturing, and killing more than one hundred thousand defenseless women and children; here was a scene in which Spanish Fascist soldiers held bayonet practice upon the living flesh of batches of fettered republican prisoners of war; here was a scene in which the thatched huddle of an African village exploded in blood beneath a rain of Italian bombs; here was a scene in which German storm troopers looted, burned, and murdered their way through a helpless Jewish ghetto; here was a scene in which thousands of political prisoners miserably perished in a slave-labor camp (was it Nazi or Stalinist?—no matter); here were scenes in which entire democratic nations were conquered by foreign aggressors without a shot being fired; here were scenes in which the leaders of the free world truckled and abased themselves before the boastful threats of international gangsters. And all the while, just beyond camera range, waited the forces of sanity which could put an end to all this horror—provided they were mobilized in time, before they too were overwhelmed by evil....

And worst of all about this nightmare was your realization that it was not a nightmare. For these were not scenes from some mad, fictitious scenario; the film you were watching was a newsreel.

There was a terrible inevitability about the collapse of the world order after 1930; events succeeded each other with a kind of numbing interior logic. What the elements of that logic were we have already examined in previous chapters: how the peace treaties of 1919 bred despair, hatred, and political chaos from which new tyrannies emerged; how the former Allies disarmed; how democracy was everywhere weakened by the ravages of depression; how Russia and the United States, each for different reasons, retreated from Europe and the Orient; how Japan emerged as the solitary Western-style Asiatic power; how people's minds became enslaved by totalitarian philosophies. Now we must observe how these elements combined and interacted to produce a chain reaction of worldwide catastrophe.

The drama opened, as it was to end, in the Orient. There, on September 18, 1931, Japanese Army officers in Manchuria provoked a clash with Chinese forces which gave them an excuse to conquer the entire province. For many years Japanese troops had been stationed in Manchuria under treaty agreement with China to protect the Japanese-owned South Manchurian Railway. These forces, organized into what was called the Kwantung Army, had grown disdainful and almost independent of Japanese home government control. Indeed, Japan's military leaders had already determined to put an end to party government through a carefully orchestrated campaign of terror. Their plots disrupted Japanese political life all through the twenties. Employing secret societies and civilian Right-wing fanatics, they assassinated scores of party politicians between 1921 and 1932, including the Prime Minister, Ki Tsuyoshi Inukai. Thereafter, until the end of World War II, of eleven Japanese Prime Ministers, four were admirals, four were generals, and only three were civilians—but civilians under complete military domination. This meant that from 1932 on, Japanese governments supported the overall militarist "solution" of expansion through conquest—thereafter they would argue only about the scale and timing of aggression. With this program the new Emperor Hirohito, who ascended the throne in December 1926, was in passive agreement.

This final militarization of Japan's government reflected the determination of her ruling classes to protect their autocratic position at any cost. The onset of the Great Depression in Japan in 1930 gave new impetus to democratic and socialist ideas among Japanese workers and peasants; Japan's rulers sought to discipline discontent through the exaltation of ancient martial "virtues" and to divert it through foreign conquest. Life would be glorious, they assured the suffering masses, once Japan had completed the task of enslaving her neighbors.

The implementation of this program of conquest seemed, in 1931, a matter of urgency for yet another reason. This was the fact that Sun Yat-sen's nationalist movement in China, now organized into the Kuomintang Party and led by the young General Chiang Kai-shek, was finally winning control of China. After years of bitter strife and civil war, Chiang was unifying the sleeping giant; should he succeed in rousing it from slumber and organizing its latent energies, then all Japan's ambitions in Asia would fail. In that case the domestic repercussions would probably lead to a revolution which could cost Japan's ruling clique of militarists, aristocrats, and big businessmen their positions and even their lives.

So it was absolutely necessary to halt Chiang's progress—and Manchuria was an appropriate place to start. Which was why, although the Kwantung Army acted independently (even mutinously) in 1931 when it provoked fighting there, the Japanese government acquiesced. Within a very short time the entire province had been "pacified" and, in March 1932, was proclaimed the "independent" Japanese puppet state of Manchukuo.

Two nations were deeply alarmed by these developments—Russia and the United States. Neither, however, could exercise much influence in the Orient. Russia could not because her Red Army was unprepared in the Far East. And besides, under Stalin's tutelage the Soviet instrument in China, the Chinese Communist Party, had been shattered on the rock of Chiang Kai-shek's personal political ambitions. The remnants of the party, led by Mao Tse-tung, were now holed up in northwest China, fighting for their very lives against Chiang's nationalist forces. The United States, having scrapped its two-ocean navy years before, also lacked the military means to intervene. Herbert Hoover's Secretary of State, Henry L. Stimson, vigorously protested the Japanese aggression—and even suggested to Britain, France, and other "interested" nations a combined intervention. When this proved fruitless Stimson urged the League of Nations, of which the United States was not a member, to do something. The League did. It established a commission to investigate the matter. The commission reported back in September 1932, condemning Japan's actions. Although no concrete measures were proposed to force Japan's evacuation of Manchuria, the League's acceptance of the commission report provided the Japanese government with the excuse it sought. On March 27, 1933, Japan simply walked out of the League of Nations. During the next three years Japanese Army forces from Manchuria, using the pretexts of "suppressing disorder" and "protecting Japanese interests," infiltrated and established their control over several more northern Chinese provinces.

An interested observer of these distant events was Adolf Hitler. One could, it appeared, defy the League of Nations with impunity. Since Hitler's program embraced the utter destruction of the wobbly edifice of peace created in 1919, the Führer felt he might as well start with the League. Accordingly, in 1933 Germany also walked out. Emboldened by the ease of this maneuver, Hitler in 1934 overreached himself. In that year he encouraged the growing Austrian Nazi Party to attempt the overthrow of the Austrian government. The ultimate aim was *Anschluss* by Germany of Austria—something specifically forbidden by the Versailles treaties. Although they managed to murder Austrian Premier Engelbert Dollfuss, the Viennese Nazis were put down by the Austrian Army and police. England and France delivered strong warnings to Berlin and, more to the point, Mussolini rushed Italian Army divisions to the southern Austrian border. Hitler disclaimed all knowledge of the attempted overthrow—and immediately embarked upon a policy of winning Mussolini's friendship and support. His Nazification of Germany was yet incomplete, and his rearmament program only then getting under way, Hitler felt he could do no more. In any case, he had long been an admirer of Il Duce; the two dictators had much in common and similar goals.

It may be asked why the League of Nations was so powerless in the face of Japanese and German defiance. Aside from the failings of its structure, the League, in the absence of Russia and the United States, could never be more than an international debating society. But while the United States would continue to remain aloof, Stalin in 1934 had a change of heart. He was alarmed by Hitler's move on Austria—and alarmed too by Hitler's constant tirades against Communism and repeated assertions that one day Germany would destroy the "Soviet menace." Having done as much as anyone to bring Hitler into power, Stalin awakened, too late, to the danger of Nazi aggression. In an attempt to win Russia allies against possible German attack, he finally joined the League of Nations in 1934. Soviet Foreign Minister Maksim Litvinov, long an advocate of cooperation with the Western powers, now became the strongest advocate in the League of "collective resistance" to aggression. Russia even went so far as to conclude treaties of mutual defense with France and Czechoslovakia in that same year. Furthermore, Communist parties abroad were instructed, through the Comintern, to now seek cooperation with the detested socialists and democratic parties for the creation of a "Popular Front" to oppose the spread of Nazism and fascism. As we have seen, this policy brought to power the Léon Blum government in France in 1935. It did not, however, prevent Hitler from openly repudiating, that year, those sections of the Versailles Treaty which restricted German military power. To all the world Hitler announced an unlimited expansion of German military might. Although German rearmament had been progressing stealthily for years, it now moved into high gear.

Nor did the Popular Front policy prevent Mussolini from attacking Ethiopia (Abyssinia) in 1935. The last independent African nation, Ethiopia had badly defeated a previous Italian aggression in 1896. To wipe out the stain of that old humiliation, to "blood" his new armies, to expand Italy's African Empire, and to grab Ethiopian raw materials for Italian industry, Mussolini—the man who had been jailed several times for opposing Italian imperialism in Africa—launched his modern legions against the ill-organized, poorly armed people of that hapless land. With their towns and villages obliterated by Italian bombers, their armies mowed down by Italian machine guns and overrun by

Italian tanks against which they could oppose little more than muskets and spears, Ethiopians turned to the League of Nations for help.

England, alarmed by the establishment of Italian power upon the vital Red Sea route to India and the East—her "lifeline of Empire"—proposed that the member nations of the League adopt economic sanctions against Italy. This idea was supported by France, Russia, and several other nations. But the economic sanctions dutifully adopted by the League—mainly a boycott on the sale of arms, oil, and other supplies to Italy—were never really enforced. When Ethiopian Emperor Haile Selassie personally addressed the League Assembly in Geneva, pleading for help, he was laughed and shouted down by a mob of Italian journalists who were covering the proceedings. Within a year Ethiopia became a part of Mussolini's new Roman Empire.

The year 1936 brought new horrors and tensions to the international scene. For in July of that year began the single most passionate struggle of this century, the Spanish Civil War. Just five years earlier, after centuries of tolerating royal misrule, the Spanish people had driven their king into exile and proclaimed a Republic. The revolution was bloodless—but not its aftermath. The Spanish people, like Italians, Germans, and others, had no experience of democratic government. They were also possessed of a cultural heritage of extremism and violence. All the "isms" that troubled the rest of the world and a few peculiarly Spanish besides divided Spaniards with a passion and ferocity unknown in other lands. Anarchists, Stalinists, Trotskyists, socialists of several varieties, liberals, conservatives, monarchists, fascists, local separatists, clericalists, and anticlericalists battled in strikes, riots, assassinations, plots, and all kind of mischiefs to win control of the Republic. Because of an almost feudal agrarian society preserved in the countryside well into the twentieth century, and an urban industrialization managed like a Dickensian nightmare, Spain lacked the middle-class economic and social foundations of democracy. The fiery Spanish temper kept the Republic in a constant state of uproar until finally, in 1936, a conspiracy of generals, fascists, monarchists, and bishops raised the standard of open rebellion.

The leader of this military uprising (his rivals for that post all died in mysterious "accidents") was General Francisco Franco-Bahamonde. Although adopting the political coloration of the Spanish fascist party, the Falange, Franco, it soon developed, was simply in the ancient tradition of Spanish strong men. His program was not really fascist—he wished only to freeze Spanish society into sixteenth-century forms. Since he enjoyed the support of the professional army, the national police force called the *Guardia Civil*, the Moorish legions from Spain's North African colonies, and the Catholic Church, it at first appeared that his victory would be swift.

But the masses of the Spanish people submerged their differences temporarily to unite in support of their Republic. Citizens militias were hastily organized by the various Left-wing and centrist political parties, and these, although they had no training and few arms, held control of Madrid, Barcelona, Valencia, and fully two thirds of the rest of the country after the initial shock.

Facing a long and now problematical struggle, Franco dispatched emissaries to Mussolini and Hitler begging for help. Il Duce, his triumphant armies now returning from their conquest of Ethiopia, enthusiastically rushed planes, arms, and entire divisions of troops to help establish a new fascist regime on the Mediterranean. The Führer, cautious about arousing English and French wrath, sent arms, expert advisors, and several squadrons of planes organized into the Kondor Legion. While welcoming the creation of a client dictatorship on France's southwestern border, he was, perhaps, more interested in testing the German Army's new weapons and tactics.

The republican government appealed to England, France, the United States, and the Soviet Union for aid. As the legal government of Spain it was fully entitled to do so. But France and England, fearing to engage in an open struggle against Mussolini which might drive him irretrievably into Hitler's embrace, refused. The United States, bound by Congressional neutrality, legislation, and wide-spread isolationist sentiment, also declared itself neutral. Only Russia agreed to send supplies, arms, and experts (but no troops) to help the Republic. Stalin's motives in this were hardly altruistic. He was pleased to maintain a fighting front in Spain which would absorb some, at least, of the German military energies; he was also anxious to test out the equipment and tactics of the Red Army. Mostly he hoped that by involving the democracies as Soviet allies with the Spanish Republic, he could strengthen the Popular Front movement against the Nazi threat to Russia itself. Employing the resources of the Comintern, Stalin was also able to recruit the famed International Brigades—composed of volunteers from every nation, irrespective of political allegiances, to help fight fascism. The Spanish Civil War soon developed into a proxy rehearsal for World War II.

England and France attempted to curb German and

Italian aid to Franco, and Russian aid to the Republic, by luring them into a Nonintervention Committee. The dictators, who had no intention of actually complying with any rules the committee might adopt, readily agreed. Thereafter, despite the participation of the Italian Navy, the Italian Army, and elements of the German war machine on Franco's side, and continued shipments of arms and experts from Russia to the Republic, the fiction of international neutrality was maintained. Because Russia could not, and, as we shall see, would not, match fascist aid, the nonintervention policy worked almost entirely to Franco's advantage and assured him of eventual triumph. The British were not entirely blind to all this—British policy was more subtle than that. Above all, the British government wished to avoid a general European war for which neither her people nor her armed forces were prepared. Prime Minister Stanley Baldwin and his successor, Neville Chamberlain, realized that if none of the major powers were *publicly* committed to the victory of either side in Spain, the chances of war were greatly lessened.

And so the fighting in Spain continued. Since Stalin's aim was not a republican victory but rather the prolongation of the fighting to keep the Nazis and Fascists engaged, he never sent the Republic the aid with which they might have triumphed. Later he would employ the Spanish Communist Party as his personal weapon to destroy Spanish Trotskyists, anarchists, and socialists—even at the price of wrecking republican chances for survival. As always, he remained sensitive to the emergence of rival Left-wing leaders abroad.

While their governments remained "neutral," the peoples of the democracies became fiercely involved from afar. For there, on the burning plains of Spain, the various ideologies of the twentieth century took on solid shape and form and fought themselves out. The muddy motives of national greed, fighting for mere survival, and ignoble imperialist aims that had marked the World War seemed not to apply to Spain. There men fought for ideals. As a republican deputy proclaimed over the radio from besieged Madrid: "Here in Madrid is the universal frontier that separates liberty and slavery.... This is Madrid. It is fighting for Spain, for Humanity, for Justice, and with the mantle of its blood, it shelters all human beings. Madrid! Madrid!" For those who remember it, the final defeat of the Republic in March 1939 was a tragedy incomparably more moving than any other event of a shameful decade.

The struggle in Spain was barely three months old when Hitler took a wild gamble: He sent German Army units to reoccupy the demilitarized Rhineland. A wild gamble because this was a move that directly threatened French security, and as the worried German General Staff pointed out, the still-forming, still-arming German war machine could offer no resistance at all if the French decided to march. France's Army of three million men was still accounted the strongest by far in all the world; it could easily brush aside German resistance and parade its way to Berlin itself if France so wished. Hitler insisted, however, that he had taken the measure of the democracies in Spain and Ethiopia; they were too decadent, too cowardly to fight.

The event proved the Führer correct. The French ordered partial mobilization and prepared to act; but England refused to support her ally. And since the basic cornerstone of all French policy was never to go to war without the support of the British Empire, France contented herself with a diplomatic protest over this new violation of the Versailles Treaty. In an England unprepared for war it was felt that the Germans were, after all, only reoccupying their own territory from which they had been unwisely and, perhaps unjustly, excluded at French insistence by the Versailles Treaty. Hitler, overjoyed at his easy success, immediately proclaimed his undying love of peace and even offered to enter into nonaggression treaties with any and all nations. Alarm in France soon subsided. Yet the French had suffered a disastrous defeat. For Germany was now able to construct a fortress line on her French frontier which, held by relatively few troops, could prevent the French Army from invading the Fatherland. This in turn meant that France would be unable to come to the assistance of those Eastern European countries, such as Poland and Czechoslovakia, with whom she had concluded militiary treaties designed to discourage German aggression.

In the autumn of 1936, impressed by solid evidence of growing German power and contemptuous of the weakness displayed by Britain and France over events in Ethiopia and Spain, Mussolini journeyed to Germany to conclude an alliance with Hitler. This took the form of Italy's promise to adhere to the so-called Anti-Comintern Pact which had been signed by Germany and Japan a year earlier. The agreement supposedly bound the signatories only to combat Communist subversion. Secret provisions, however, included a mutual-defense treaty against Russian aggression. Calling it merely an anti-Comintern instrument would, the dictators knew, win approval among those political groups in the democracies whose fear of Communism outweighed all other considerations. Mussolini bombastically described his agreements with Hitler as creating a new political "axis" around which all of Europe would henceforth revolve.

Meantime, in distant Asia, Japanese militarism re-

sumed its march. Kwantung Army officers, on maneu-
vers near Peking, provoked an armed clash with
Chinese soldiers guarding the Marco Polo Bridge near
the old Imperial capital on July 7, 1937. The Japanese
government, headed by Prime Minister Prince Konoye
Fumimaro, a supposedly "liberal" civilian, seized upon
this minor occurrence and subsequent anti-Japanese
rioting in Chinese cities to launch a full-scale attack
upon Chiang Kai-shek's nationalist regime. Japanese
forces captured Peking, subdued Shanghai, and began
the methodical conquest of huge areas of northern and
coastal China. On December 13, 1937, they captured
the nationalist capital of Nanking—and went berserk
in an orgy of rape and murder that shocked the world.
Yet despite the fact that their armies plunged deeper
and deeper into China against poorly armed and poorly
led nationalist forces, the Japanese government refused to declare war. A state of war would immediately
bring into force American neutrality legislation, which
would lead to the cutting off of vital American sales of
scrap iron and oil to Japan. For the next eight years,
Japanese governments would refer to the endless fighting on the mainland as the "China Incident."

When Chiang Kai-shek appealed to the League of
Nations for help, that august body issued a mild condemnation of Japanese aggression. As for the Americans—Roosevelt made a speech in October 1937 in
which he proposed that the "peace-loving nations" join
forces to "quarantine the aggressors." But this drew no
positive response from England or France, while it did
produce a flood of frightened, angry letters from Americans determined that their sons should never again
be sent to fight in "foreign wars." Even when two
months later Japanese planes deliberately bombed and
sank the American gunboat *Panay* which was peace-

fully patroling China's Yangtse River, American opinion could not be aroused. A Japanese apology for the "mistake" and the payment of reparations quickly resolved the incident.

In February 1938 Hitler, with a German Army and especially its air force, the *Luftwaffe,* immeasurably stronger than the days of his "wild gamble" in the Rhineland, decided the time had come to proceed with Austrian *Anschluss.* Unlike the situation during his first attempt in 1934, this time the political alignments made Mussolini an ally rather than an adversary—and in the intervening period the Austrian Nazi Party had grown in strength and belligerence. Once again Austrian Nazis were instructed to demonstrate, march, and riot to produce political chaos. Then the Austrian Premier, Kurt von Schuschnigg, was summoned to the Führer's private retreat at Berchtesgaden in the Bavarian Alps, where he was subjected to a tirade of abuse about Austrian inability to maintain order and "protect the lives of innocent Germans." The tirade was followed by an ultimatum: Either Schuschnigg would turn over state power to the Austrian Nazis, or the German Army would invade his country. The Austrian Premier begged for a few weeks in which to sound out the opinions of the Austrian people. When Schuschnigg reminded Hitler that Austria was not alone in the world, the Führer scoffed—nobody, not England, France, or Italy, would lift a finger to preserve Austrian independence.

Again he was proven correct. During the days of crisis that followed, England and France confined themselves to diplomatic notes of protest against German interference in Austria. Schuschnigg, in despair, announced he would hold a plebiscite through which the Austrian people could express their views. This, of course, the Führer could not countenance; for despite all the riotous noise made by local Nazis, there could be little doubt that the overwhelming majority of the Austrian people would vote against them. Accordingly, on March 12, 1938, German armored divisions rumbled over the Austrian border and, facing no opposition, reached Vienna in a matter of hours. A few days later Austria was annexed outright to the Third Reich.

If the German General Staff had been worried about possible Anglo-French intervention in the Rhineland in 1936, many of its officers were even more frightened of the possible consequences of the Anschluss of 1938. The German Army and the Luftwaffe were stronger, yes—but they were still no match for the huge French Army. The tanks of the German armored divisions broke down continuously on the road to Vienna, and the infantry regiments were still underequipped and undertrained. Yet by now it was perfectly apparent that Hitler meant to conquer all of Europe eventually. If not over Austria, then over Czechoslovakia, Poland, or some other of the Führer's targets, the French and English were bound to go to war. The Soviet Union would undoubtedly side with them and, eventually, even the United States. Germany could never win such a war—it would bring utter disaster. So various of the German generals, along with Admiral Wilhelm Canaris, head of German Intelligence, and certain civilians, began to plot Hitler's overthrow. Their conspiracy, which would later be dubbed the *Schwartze Kapelle* or Black Choir by the Nazi secret police, began, in 1938, to send secret information to the British Government, warning of Hitler's plans. Should England and France stand up to the Führer's threats, that would provoke a crisis in Germany. Then, the conspirators said, they would be able to arrest Hitler, seize the government,

The Destruction of Versailles

Hitler's "Peaceful Expansion,"
1935–1939.

Italy's Conquest of Albania,
1939.

Russian Expansion,
1939–1941.

and overthrow Nazi tyranny. British Intelligence chiefs questioned the authenticity of these communications while the British government largely discounted them. Nonetheless, the anti-Nazi plotters continued to organize and bided their time.

Following his conquest of Austria, Hitler had once again filled the air with promises of everlasting peace—but rapidly prepared to fall upon his next victim, Czechoslovakia. He employed many of the same weapons he had used against Austria. The Treaty of Versailles had given Czechoslovakia dominion over some three million Germans living along the mountainous German border in the Sudetenland. These had long since been organized into a local Nazi Party. On instructions from Berlin the Sudeten Nazis now began a campaign of political disruption and complaint about the "cruel treatment" they received at the hands of the Czech government. They yearned, they said, to rejoin their Fatherland. Hitler announced that he would rescue them.

But Czechoslovakia was not Austria. The Czech army was one of the best, and best armed, in Europe—in 1938 its strength was about equal to that of the German Army. Furthermore it held naturally defensible positions along the German frontier. Moreover, Czechoslovakia was a very real and vibrantly progressive democracy whose well-educated citizens were determined to defend their freedom. Finally, Czechoslovakia enjoyed military alliances with France and with the Soviet Union. It would not be an easy nut to crack, even for Hitler.

The Führer, however, confident that he could once again win without war, while fully determined to fight if he had to, went boldly ahead with his plans. He instructed his Army chiefs to prepare for an invasion

of Czechoslovakia on October 1, 1938. When they protested the dangers of his plan, he pointed out that work
on the so-called Westwall along the French border was
now far advanced—the French would be unable to pen-
etrate it; German armies now outflanked the Czech
defenses from their new positions in Austria; Russian
aid could reach the Czechs only through Poland, which
would never cooperate with the Soviets; and the French
and English would once again back down before the
threat of war. Some of the generals present at this
lecture, secret members of the Schwartze Kapelle, felt
certain that now, at least, the Führer had overreached
himself and their hour was at hand.

In the end it was, as Wellington said of Waterloo,
"a close-run thing." The summer of 1938 was one prolonged international crisis. While diplomats scurried
between European capitals, the British Royal Navy
went to battle stations and the French Army partially
mobilized. Antiaircraft batteries and air-raid shelters
made their appearances in London and Paris, while gas
masks were distributed to civilians. Russia announced
that she would honor her treaty with Czechoslovakia
provided France did—and provided the Poles allowed
her troops to pass through their country. But at the
very last minute war was avoided. For on September
29 British Prime Minister Neville Chamberlain and
French Premier Édouard Daladier joined Hitler and
Mussolini in Munich to negotiate a settlement. As
Hitler had predicted, the Poles would permit no Russians to pass through their country, and neither the
French nor the British were prepared to fight over what
Chamberlain described as "a quarrel in a faraway country between people of whom we know nothing." By the
terms of the Munich Agreement, Czechoslovakia was
forced to hand over to Germany the entire Sudeten

territory—if she refused, warned the British and French, she would face Hitler alone. This dismemberment left the Czechs defenseless—and added to the German war machine the great Czech Skoda arms plant. As Hitler had planned all along, German forces entered Czech territory on October 1.

In return for this act of British and French appeasement, the Führer swore to Chamberlain that he had "no further territorial ambitions in Europe." His aim, after all, was merely the reuniting of Germans, and that was now accomplished. He would certainly respect the new, diminished Czech frontiers—and would even join Britain and France in guaranteeing them forever. Peace would now prevail. Chamberlain believed him and, when he returned to cheering throngs in London, declared: ". . . There has come back from Germany to Downing Street peace with honor. I believe it is peace for our time." In the House of Commons the lonely voice of Winston Churchill warned: "We have sustained a great defeat without a war, the consequences of which will travel far with us." The conspirators of the Schwartze Kapelle threw up their hands in despair. "What can you do with h'm [Hitler]?" demanded General Ludwig Beck. "He succeeds in everything he does!"

Hitler waited only six months before breaking his word again; he was determined to devour the rest of Czechoslovakia. This he accomplished by first provoking the usual riots—on the part of Slovaks against Czechs. He then invited the Slovaks to set up their own autonomous government. When the Czechs attempted to put down this rebellion, Hitler had his excuse. He summoned the feeble old Czech Prime Minister, Emil Hacha, to Berlin and presented him with an ultimatum: Either Czechoslovakia would sign an agreement incorporating itself into the Third Reich or German troops and planes would conquer the country. Hacha, chased around the conference table by Göring waving a pen, collapsed. He was revived by an injection given by Hitler's personal physician. Befuddled and terrified, the old man signed. On March 16, 1939, the German Army occupied Prague. Czechoslovakia had ceased to exist.

At first it seemed that Chamberlain would swallow this affront meekly, as he had all the others. But opinion in Britian, both official and public, was outraged by this final evidence of Hitler's perfidy. In a speech at Birmingham on March 18, Chamberlain denounced the latest German aggression and, on March 31, speaking in the House of Commons, revealed that Britain and France had extended a joint "guarantee" to the Poles to help them against any German invasion, it being obvious that Poland was next on the Führer's list of victims.

There was, of course, no way British or French forces could reach Poland to give real effect to that promise; only the Russians could provide immediate support. So an Anglo-French mission was dispatched to Moscow to explore the possibility of a military alliance with the Soviet Union. Progress toward such an agreement was, however, painfully slow.

Even before his final rape of Czechoslovakia, Hitler had begun his campaign against Poland. He demanded the return of Danzig and the Polish Corridor, which separated East Prussia from the rest of Germany. Poland, still ruled by the nationalistic military caste installed after the World War, rejected the Führer's demands contemptuously. The Polish generals were confident that they could repulse any German attack. So confident were they, and so blind to realities, that they also contemptuously rejected the possibility of

Russian aid. Not a single Soviet soldier would be permitted, they declared, to set foot on Polish soil. This, of course, crippled Allied negotiations in Moscow. How, demanded the Russians, were they expected to help the Poles? How, for that matter, did the Allies expect to help the Poles? Meanwhile, during the spring and summer of 1939, Hitler orchestrated his usual propaganda war: The fiendish Poles were persecuting and torturing their helpless German minority—it was Germany's duty to rescue them.

As tension mounted, the world was briefly distracted by Mussolini's sudden descent upon tiny Albania. Jealous of Hitler's bloodless victories, Il Duce seized the small kingdom across the Adriatic to remind the democracies that he too was an important conqueror.

From the battlements of the Kremlin Stalin had closely followed events in the West, even during the distractions of his domestic purges. These bloody mass killings, punctuated between 1936 and 1939 by a series of "show trials" during which the defendants always publicly confessed, had effectively wiped out all the so-called Old Bolsheviks, thousands of dissident intellectuals, and most of the higher officer corps of the Red Army. All were accused of plotting with the fascist and/or democratic powers to overthrow the Communist paradise. By 1939 Stalin, secure at home, had reached certain conclusions about realities on the international front. In the Anglo-French appeasement policy he saw two obvious factors: The Western democracies evidently hoped to turn Hitler's wrath to the East and, in any event, were too decadent and cowardly to stand up to the Nazis. The Popular Front policy had failed—Russia would have to face Hitler alone. If that was true, she would do so on her own terms. Maksim Litvinov, the friend of the West, was replaced as Foreign

Minister by Vyacheslav M. Molotov, a hard-nosed Stalinist.

Hitler was well aware of this shift in Soviet foreign policy. He was also aware that his generals feared, above all, the possibility of a two-front war. Although confident that the French and English would abandon Poland as they had abandoned Austria and Czechoslovakia, the Führer, with the ruthlessness possible to an absolute dictator, determined to allay the worries of his General Staff which he shared. Beginning in July 1939 the Führer entered into secret negotiations with Stalin. What did it matter that he had spent twenty years denouncing Communism in the most bloodthirsty terms? His followers would realize that any agreement with Russia was a temporary expedient—that Germany's future still lay in an eventual *Drang nach Osten.* Anyhow, who in the Third Reich would dare to publicly protest this apparent abandonment of the most cherished and loudly proclaimed Nazi "ideals"? On August 24, 1939, the world learned, to its stunned dismay and disbelief, that the two former archenemies, Nazi Germany and Soviet Russia, had signed a Non-Aggression Pact. By its public terms, each side promised not to attack the other in the event of a European war, and both sides agreed to a huge expansion of trade. With his eastern front now secure, and a flow of Russian food and raw materials assured, an elated Hitler confirmed his orders: The attack on Poland would begin within a week.

And so the decade approached its end with Anglo-French policy in ruins and war all but certain. Why, it may be asked, did the European democracies, with the power to stop Hitler at any time up to, say, 1938, continually appease him, thereby creating the very monster they most dreaded? Primarily because the

French and English people themselves, with the horrors of the World War still fresh in memory, would have gone to almost any lengths to avoid another conflict, especially one to support what were widely perceived as the *unjust* provisions of the Versailles Treaty. And, too, Stalin was right—powerful political circles in France and England hoped that Hitler could be led into attacking the Soviet Union; that way the two dictators could devour each other. There was also the fact that Western leaders, especially Chamberlain, unused to dealing with gangsters, really believed Hitler's reiterated promises that each bloodless conquest would be his last. And, finally, the Great Depression had crippled military budgets in the West for many years; neither England nor France felt prepared to fight. As for the United States, although Roosevelt saw and warned of the approaching peril, the overwhelming majority of Americans cherished isolationist sentiments and the belief that they were insulated from European problems by the Atlantic Ocean. It was one public-opinion battle that FDR could not win for the present.

In assessing the shambles of democratic policy between the wars, American foreign-affairs expert and historian George F. Kennan was to observe:

"In 1917, the Western Powers, in their determination to inflict total defeat on a Germany far less dangerous to them than that of Hitler, had pressed so unwisely for the continuation of Russia's help that they consigned her to the arms of the Communists. Now, in 1939, they were paying the price for this folly.

"In 1917, they had cultivated an image of the German Kaiser that was indistinguishable from the reality of the future Hitler. Now they had a real Hitler before them.

"In 1917, they convinced themselves that Russia's

help was essential to their victory, though this was not really true. Now they had a situation in which Russia's help was indeed essential; but the Russia they needed was not there.

"You see in this example what happens when people make policy on the basis of exaggerated fears and prejudices. Those dangers they conjure up in their own imagination eventually take on flesh and rise to assail them—or if not them, then their children. And they waste, in their over-anxiety before the fancied perils of the present, the assets they will need for the real ones of the future."

On September 1, 1939, the German war machine crashed across the Polish frontier. Two days later that event occurred which had been the suppressed nightmare of the world since 1918: England and France declared war on Germany. The twenty-year Armistice was at an end.

> *It struck me suddenly, with unmistakable clarity,*
> *that I had stumbled on a secret locked within*
> *the Führer's breast, a secret he would never*
> *let out and which he may never admit having.*
> *Hitler by instinct feared Franklin D. Roosevelt.*

PIERRE HUSS
American journalist

10

Short of War

"I cannot go any faster than the people will let me," Franklin D. Roosevelt once patiently explained to a supporter urging haste. To a man who so well remembered Woodrow Wilson's tragic fight for the League, the possibility of one day looking back over his shoulder to discover that he had no followers was an ever-present nightmare. FDR could use his high office to cajole, educate, reason with the American people; he never felt he could use it to impose ideas for which they were unprepared. Which was, perhaps, the chief reason why the twenty-seven months of American neutrality that followed Europe's plunge into war represented a special kind of agony for the President.

FDR knew—had known since 1936 at least—that Nazism and fascism were mortal threats to the American way of life. His leadership had outflanked and baffled totalitarian voices at home, but had been unable to prevent their rise to power abroad. The American people, convinced that they had been tricked into the First World War, disillusioned by the failure of the ideals for which they had fought, cynical about European motives, and distraught by their own problems, would not support any initiatives FDR might have employed to stop the dictators before 1939. For that matter, neither would the leaders of England and France; to FDR's proposals for joint action in the years before the war, Chamberlain returned a cold and indifferent response. Reflecting the opinions of the electorate, Congress had passed several different measures, lumped together in the public mind as the Neutrality Acts, designed to prevent any possible American participation in foreign conflicts. FDR had been able in 1934 to reestablish normal diplomatic relations with the Soviet Union, but only because it was hoped that this might increase trade—it did not—and thereby help alleviate the Depression, not because any alliance against fascism was sought. Now the catastrophe FDR had feared and predicted had come—and most Americans still considered it none of their business.

Well, perhaps not quite "none of their business," because now, with French and English orders for munitions, arms, and supplies pouring in to American industry, business was rapidly improving. Despite the heroic efforts of the New Deal, the Great Depression in America was ended not by reform but by the booming prosperity of war. It was, in fact, quite fascinating to observe how neutrality laws were relaxed, step by step, to safeguard not American vital interests but rather the huge profits of American trade with the Allies. After a decade of impoverishment the American people were back at work again—and they wanted nothing to disturb their enjoyment of a long-delayed prosperity. Secure in the belief that they were completely protected by wide oceans, most Americans followed the news from Europe with somewhat less interest than they did that of their local baseball teams.

The news from Europe was startling. Hitler's war machine, displaying new weapons and tactics—mainly long, speedy thrusts by mechanized armored divisions employed in conjunction with tactical air power—conquered the overconfident Poles in the first three weeks of September 1939. It was, boasted the Germans, *Blitzkrieg* or lightning war. But before the swastika waved over Warsaw, some of the secret terms of the German-Soviet pact were revealed when the Red Army invaded Poland from the east, ending all hope of Polish resistance and recovering for Russia the territory Poland had won from her in 1920. Other secret provisions of the pact were revealed in subsequent months when Soviet forces entered Lithuania, Latvia, and Estonia, stamping out the independence of these Versailles-created Baltic nations.

With Poland conquered, Hitler's occupation forces commenced a savage, methodical extermination campaign not only against Poland's three million Jews but also against her ruling classes. Military, political, and labor leaders, intellectuals, teachers, business leaders—all those around whom resistance to Nazi rule might form—were murdered *en masse*. Poles were to be no more than expendable slaves for the Third Reich. Although millions perished at the hands of Nazi execution squads and in bestial concentration camps, little or no news of these massacres reached the West. Not that such news is likely to have had any appreciable effect in the Western democracies anyhow: For ten years the Nazis had been degrading, torturing, and exterminating German Jews in the face of worldwide indifference. While public opinion in the democracies was certainly revolted by Hitler's war against the Jews, it was not so strongly revolted as to provoke more than diplomatic protests on the part of democratic governments. The terrible murder factories, the death camps of the Holocaust which would consume nearly ten million Europeans, of whom six million were Jews, were not yet established—but their coming was clearly foreshadowed by the dark night of horror which fell upon prostrate Poland in the autumn of 1939.

While Poland was extinguished, Anglo-French forces in the west adopted a defensive posture. The British Royal Navy established a long-range blockade of Germany, and a British Expeditionary Force took up its positions along the Belgian border while the French Army manned its Maginot Line facing Germany. This complex, powerful string of underground fortifications had been constructed between the wars by a French General Staff determined to avoid another bloodletting like that of 1914–1919. Let the Germans hurl themselves to pieces against these impenetrable defenses— secure behind them, France would conserve her manhood. So passive were both the Allied and German forces facing each other in the west during the first seven months of the war that Americans dubbed the conflict a *"Sitzkrieg"*—a sitting war. While French and German soldiers hung their washing out to dry on the guns of their respective fortifications—the Germans now called theirs the Siegfried Line—Allied politicians congratulated each other that Hitler feared to attack. Winston Churchill, now again, as in 1914, First Lord of the Admiralty, waged a vigorous sea campaign against German surface raiders and U-boats, but the only bellicose activity to disturb the peace on land was a Russian attack upon Finland in November 1939. Since Finland had been the only European country to make regular payments on her American loans, this especially irritated American public opinion. "Plucky little Finland" surprised and delighted the world when she hurled back the first Red Army offensives—but by March 1940 she was forced to surrender.

Then, in April 1940, the German war machine overran Denmark and attacked Norway. "Hitler," a beaming Chamberlain informed Parliament, "has missed the bus." But within a matter of days it was seen that the Royal Navy could not cut off the daring German assault forces because it could not defend itself against the Luftwaffe. British troops, landed on the Norwegian coast to evict the German airborne regiments, were soon driven back into the sea. Two more nations fell to the Nazy tyranny.

American opinion had barely recovered from this shock when Hitler launched his all-out attack in the west on May 10, 1940. German airborne and infantry forces invaded Holland and Belgium—and when Anglo-French divisions raced forward to meet them, powerful German *Panzer* (tank) armies crashed across the French border through the Ardennes Forest, thus skirting the "impregnable" but *unfinished* Maginot Line. The British and French armies in Belgium were cut off and trapped when the Nazi tank columns reached the English Channel. Although the British were able to evacuate some three hundred thousand of their own and French troops through the Channel port of Dunkerque, they lost all their equipment.

Meantime, the fumbling Chamberlain had been replaced as British Prime Minister by Winston Churchill. In Parliament the terrible words of Oliver Cromwell were hurled at him: "You have sat here too long for any good you have done. Depart, I say! In the name of God, go!" After the defeat in Belgium, however, Churchill had little left but his mastery of English eloquence with which to defy Hitler. He sent words into battle like armies, to bluff the Führer, enlist American help, and above all to keep ablaze the spirit of resistance among his own countrymen.

Having conquered Belgium and Holland and expelled the British from the continent, the Nazi armies now turned south to destroy the remaining, disorganized French forces. French Premier Paul Reynaud broadcast a pitiful plea to Roosevelt begging for "clouds of airplanes"—which did not exist. On June 10 Mussolini, eager to share in the spoils of an already defeated France, declared war upon the Allies. FDR told the American people: "The hand that held the dagger has struck it into the back of its neighbor, France." While Italian armies in the south got precisely nowhere, German Panzer armies swept down upon Paris and beyond.

On June 20, 1940, in that same railroad car in the forest of Compiègne where Marshal Foch had dictated the terms of the Armistice to the Kaiser's Germany (the French had preserved it as a national monument), France surrendered unconditionally to Hitler. A rump state—a fragment of the original government—ruled from Vichy by the aging, defeatist Marshal Henri Pétain was all that remained of France.

Americans were aghast at the swiftness and totality of the Allied collapse. Now, suddenly, the only thing that stood between an unarmed and unprepared America and the triumphant Nazis was the Royal Navy and

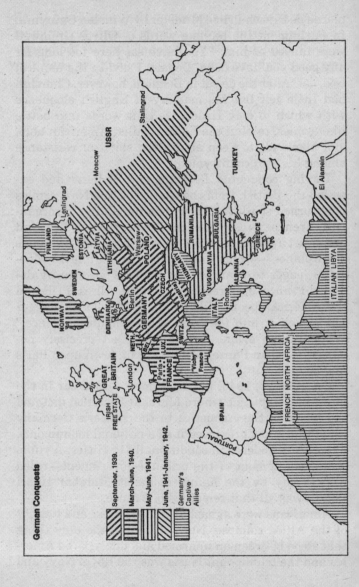

German Conquests

- September, 1939.
- March–June, 1940.
- May–June, 1941.
- June, 1941–January, 1942.
- Germany's Captive Allies

an England without weapons. How long could it take
Hitler's powerful hordes to bring Britain to her knees?
Churchill might declare, "We shall fight on the beaches,
we shall fight on the landing grounds, we shall fight
in the fields...we shall never surrender, and even
if...these islands or a large part of them should be
subjugated and starving,'then the British Empire beyond the seas, armed and guarded by the British fleet,
would continue the struggle until, in God's good time,
the New World, in all its power and might, steps forth
to the rescue and liberation of the Old," but most
Americans expected a quick Nazi victory. So alarmed
was American opinion that when FDR at Churchill's
urgent behest stripped American armories to rush
shiploads of old Springfield rifles to England, he had
to do so secretly.

Aside from his own oratorical powers and scanty
American aid, Churchill possessed one important
weapon—a weapon so vital that its very existence
would not be revealed for more than thirty years: His
cryptographers had broken the German codes. Both
Germany and Japan employed an electric coding machine known as Enigma. In the months before the war,
British mathematicians and engineers had constructed
a unique kind of primitive computer which could du-
plicate Enigma communications. Called Colossus, this
remarkable device became increasingly reliable until,
by late summer 1940, the English were able to inter-
cept and read the most highly secret German orders
and messages almost as soon as they were issued. To
supplement these intercepts (code-named Ultra) there
was also a steady flow of information from Admiral
Canaris and the Schwarze Kapelle. So tight was security surrounding Ultra and the Canaris connection
that Churchill could not, at first, disclose these sources

even to Roosevelt. This was somewhat ironic because American cryptographers were, in 1939, completing work on a similar device called Magic, with which they would soon break the Japanese Enigma codes. Of course, both Ultra and Magic intercepts had to be used with the greatest discretion—for if the Germans or Japanese ever suspected that their "impenetrable" Enigma system had been cracked, they would shift to other coding methods. Sometimes, unfortunately, great discretion had to mean ignoring the information—and a subsequent inevitable loss of lives.

It was with Ultra information as well as with their newly developed radar system and high-performance Spitfire fighter planes that the Royal Air Force was able to defeat the Luftwaffe's air offensive over Britain in the autumn of 1940. Unable to win control of English skies, Hitler postponed indefinitely his plans for an invasion of Britain—and turned his interest once again to the east.

Meanwhile, FDR's frustration deepened. Convinced that Britain's survival was essential to America's, and aware that the hope of eventual American involvement in the struggle was one of the pillars of English morale, Roosevelt had to proceed with the greatest caution in both his public and secret support of Britain. He felt able, for example, to publicly announce in August 1940 that fifty overage American destroyers had been given to the Royal Navy in return for American leases to construct military bases upon certain British Caribbean islands—but he kept secret the fact that worldwide headquarters of Britain's complex secret intelligence and underground warfare services had been established in New York's Rockefeller Center. Nor did he reveal that shortly thereafter British secret research materials and personnel—including vital infor-

mation regarding the development of an atomic bomb—
had been transferred to the United States.

For 1940 was a presidential election year—and FDR,
running for an unprecedented third term, was faced
with powerful opposition. The Republican candidate,
Wendell Willkie, was possessed of intelligence and a
kind of rugged charisma. He also enjoyed the backing
of a great body of American opinion determined to keep
the United States absolutely neutral. The voices of
isolationism were many and powerful. Colonel Charles
Lindbergh, the hero of the twenties, warned audiences
that Germany was unbeatable; the many newspapers
of William Randolph Hearst insisted that America
could "do business with Hitler"; senators and representatives, especially from the Midwest, insisted on a
policy of "America First." So fearful were many Americans of becoming entangled in the war that FDR felt
constrained to promise them during the campaign of
1940 that "your boys are not going to be sent into any
foreign wars." That this was a promise he could not
keep Roosevelt was well aware; that he had to make
it nevertheless is a measure of how powerful were the
sentiments of neutrality. It was only after he had won
the election that FDR, in January 1941, authorized the
beginning of secret military staff talks and planning
with the British.

If American aid to Britain was opposed by isolationists and America Firsters, it was also questioned by
American military leaders worried about supplying
their own rapidly expanding forces. Impelled by the
shock of Hitler's victories in the west, Congress had,
during the summer of 1940, reluctantly accepted the
President's proposal that a new draftee Army be raised.
Under the terms of the Selective Service Act which was
to run for just one year, for the first time in American

history her young men were training for war in a time of peace. They were training with broomsticks for rifles and automobiles representing tanks. Simultaneously the Army Air Corps was being hurriedly expanded and a "two-ocean Navy" constructed. Thus American needs competed with British for the still-inadequate supply of arms and munitions trickling from the American war industry. Yet it would be years before American forces were ready to fight; and if Britain was defeated in the meantime, their fight might well be a losing battle.

It was to assure the flow of supplies to Britain that FDR, in February 1941, pushed through Congress by slim majorities the Lend-Lease Act. Aware that England was near bankruptcy, and aware too of American public bitterness over the unpaid Allied war debts of 1918, Roosevelt devised a system whereby American assistance would be "lent" to Britain—some of the equipment to be presumably returned at a later date—and some to be paid for by British supplies, expertise, and other matériel. The repayment provisions of Lend-Lease were kept vague enough to satisfy American opinion while assuring a continuing flow of supplies to Britain. The United States must become, FDR declared, "the great arsenal of democracy."

When, during the following months, the German U-boat campaign in the North Atlantic grew to such tremendous proportions that it threatened to cut the vital Anglo-American supply lifeline, Roosevelt issued secret orders to the United States Navy to cooperate with the Royal Navy in the protection of trans-Atlantic convoys. This led, inevitably and increasingly, to fighting between American naval vessels and Nazi submarines. Roosevelt proceeded step by cautious step, as public opinion would allow. American ships would, he declared, "defend themselves" in their "hemispheric defense zone." Later that zone was extended to mid-Atlantic. Then, after "incidents" between U.S. patrol vessels and Nazi U-boats, he announced that American ships would "shoot on sight" any German submarine they found. American troops were dispatched to take over bases in Greenland and Iceland and, after a German U-boat torpedoed and sank the U.S. destroyer *Reuben James,* all restrictions on American naval forces were removed. But FDR was never completely frank with the American people about the role their Navy played in the North Atlantic from March to December 1941— it amounted to undeclared war against Hitler.

Meanwhile, during the autumn of 1940, a very small, ill-equipped British garrison in Egypt, under the command of General Archibald Wavell, utterly routed an invading Italian army many times its size. The new "Roman Legionnaires" fled wildly back into Italian Libya, where they surrendered by the hundreds of thousands to mere handfuls of delighted English Tommies. It was now seen how thin was the veneer of militarism that Mussolini had tried to impose upon an ancient, highly civilized people; they simply would not fight for fascism. This was even more dramatically demonstrated when in December 1940 Il Duce ordered his forces in occupied Albania to conquer neighboring Greece. The hardy Greeks promptly drove the invaders back deep into Albania itself. Soon the abashed Duce was calling upon Hitler for help.

All of which was of great interest to the Anglo-American strategists reading Ultra intercepts. For both Churchill and Roosevelt were well aware that the Führer planned to invade Russia early in 1941. They had repeatedly warned Stalin of the Nazi plan (code named Barbarossa)—only to be rebuffed. The paranoid

Soviet dictator dismissed the warnings as part of some
Allied "plot" to embroil the Soviet Union in war with
Germany. Yet it was vital that Hitler be, if not defeated, at least "contained" in Russia. How to help the
Russians accomplish this *despite* Stalin? By stirring up
enough trouble in the Balkans to lure Hitler into a
campaign in that mountainous region. The Führer's
timetable for the assault against Russia might thereby
be delayed enough so that German forces would eventually be bogged down by the harsh Russian winter.
Accordingly, FDR dispatched William ("Wild Bill")
Donovan, later chief of the American OSS, on a mission
to the Balkans which so played upon and infuriated
Hitler's temper that the Führer unleashed his Panzer
divisions against Yugoslavia and Greece in April 1941.
The German conquest of these two small nations delayed their invasion of Russia by six weeks—six weeks
which, according to the testimony of the German General Staff, cost them the opportunity of a quick decision
over Russia and hence the war itself.

Nonetheless, when on June 22, 1941, Hitler finally
unleashed his Panzer juggernaut against his former
ally, much of the Red Army and Air Force was caught
unprepared. The Nazi armies plunged deep into Russia.
Churchill immediately declared Britain's support for
the Soviet Union. "If Hitler invaded Hell," Churchill
said to an aide, "I would at least make a favorable
reference to the Devil in Parliament." Shortly thereafter FDR announced that Lend-Lease aid would be
dispatched to Russia—and faced new barrages of criticism from the many Americans whose loathing of
Communism still surpassed their fear of Hitler.

The Führer was, of course, highly sensitive to the
danger of possible American intervention in the war.
He had cautioned his U-boat commanders not to allow

themselves to be provoked, to avoid conflict with American naval vessels. And, as a counterbalance to the unofficial Anglo-American alliance, he had concluded with Mussolini and the Konoye government in Japan a so-called Tripartite Pact. Signed in September 1940, the treaty provided that should any of the three signatories be attacked by any nation *not then engaged in the European war,* the others would come to her aid. Since another article of the pact specifically excluded Russia from this provision, it was very obviously and openly directed against the United States.

Japan's adherence to the Tripartite Pact reflected the belief of her military, political, and industrial leaders that she had reached the crossroads of destiny. They were right. But trapped by the imperatives of their autocratic society and its unique history, they chose to follow the wrong route. At a meeting held on July 19, 1940, the government of Prince Konoye agreed that they should seize the opportunity offered by the Anglo-French collapse in Western Europe to proceed with the construction of the Greater East Asia Co-Prosperity Sphere. This meant expansion of the Japanese Empire to the south, at the cost of the British, French, and Dutch colonial empires. Not only would this achieve Japan's economic objectives, which could be summed up as self-sufficiency in sources of raw materials and markets, but it would also help achieve a military objective—the final conquest of China.

The "China Incident" was not going well. No matter how much Chinese territory or how many Chinese cities the Japanese armies overran, they could not seem to force a decision. The resistance of the Chiang Kaishek regime, now in uneasy alliance with Mao Tsetung's Communist forces, could not be broken. Japanese soldiers and resources were being swallowed in

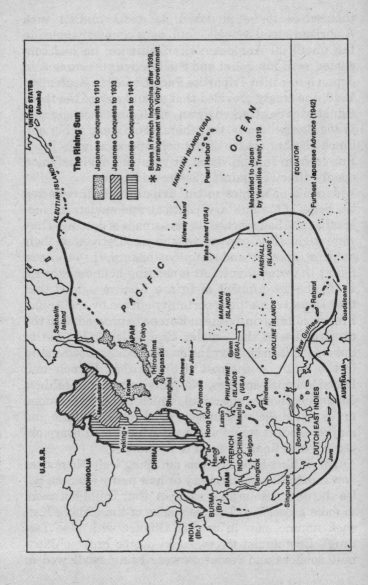

The Rising Sun

Japanese Conquests to 1910

Japanese Conquests to 1933

Japanese Conquests to 1941

* Bases in French Indochina after 1939, by arrangement with Vichy Government

Mandated to Japan by Versailles Treaty, 1919

Furthest Japanese Advance (1942)

UNITED STATES (Alaska)

ALEUTIAN ISLANDS

HAWAIIAN ISLANDS (USA)

Pearl Harbor

Midway Island

Wake Island (USA)

OCEAN

EQUATOR

PACIFIC

Sakhalin Island

JAPAN

Tokyo

Hiroshima
Nagasaki

Shanghai

Okinawa

Iwo Jima

Formosa

Hong Kong

Korea

MARSHALL ISLANDS

MARIANA ISLANDS

Guam (USA)

CAROLINE ISLANDS

New Guinea

Rabaul

Guadalcanal

U.S.S.R.

Manchukuo

Peking

CHINA

MONGOLIA

SIAM

FRENCH INDOCHINA

Hanoi

Saigon

Bangkok

BURMA (Br.)

INDIA (Br.)

Singapore

Luzon

PHILIPPINE ISLANDS (USA)

Manila

Mindanao

Borneo

DUTCH EAST INDIES

Java

AUSTRALIA

a bottomless quicksand of minor battles, skirmishes, and guerrilla warfare. Continued Chinese resistance, the Japanese believed, was based on the military (hence moral) support of the United States. American arms and supplies were reaching Chiang over the border of northern French Indochina, now called Vietnam, and along the tortuous route of the so-called Burma Road. These avenues of aid must be closed.

Obviously, Japan's plans risked war with the Western powers. Since both France and Holland had been conquered by Hitler and Britain's final defeat seemed imminent, only the United States posed a threat. But America, it was pointed out, was not yet prepared for war. Besides, the clamor being raised by American neutralists and isolationists against FDR's attempts to aid Britain convinced many in Japan that the United States might well ignore Japanese advances if these were made cautiously enough and with some legal camouflage.

In this, the Japanese leaders were badly mistaken—the lessons of earlier years were evidently forgotten. For Americans were still possessed of their ambivalent racism regarding Asia: The Chinese were still their cherished orphan wards; the Japanese were the Yellow Peril. While Americans might, in the name of neutrality, isolationism, or appeasement, bitterly denounce Roosevelt's growing intervention in the European struggle, they vigorously supported American intervention to help China—even at the risk of war. If the Japanese government did not perceive this, FDR certainly did. It emboldened him to act in the Far East with a decisive vigor he felt he could not exercise in Europe.

As early as June 1940, immediately following the Allied collapse in Europe, Japan had brought pressure to bear on British and French authorities in Southeast Asia. The English were constrained to close the Burma Road while the French colonial administrators of Indochina were forced to permit Japanese "observers" to station themselves along the Indochinese-Chinese border to prevent military supplies being smuggled across it to Chiang Kai-shek. In September 1940 the French, now obedient to the pro-Axis appeasement policies of the Vichy government, permitted the Japanese to build military airfields around Hanoi. The Japanese forces sent to "protect" these airfields amounted to a military occupation of all of northern French Indochina.

This last move, however, provoked an Anglo-American response. The British announced the reopening of the Burma Road while Roosevelt declared an embargo upon the sale of American steel and scrap iron to Japan. And when Japanese planes from Indochina began bombing and strafing American truck convoys moving along the Chinese section of the Burma Road, FDR dispatched American planes and pilots "on leave" from the Army and Marine Air Corps to fight as paid professionals in the employ of Chiang Kai-shek. Organized into a group called The Flying Tigers by "retired" American General Claire Chennault, these mercenary squadrons began taking a heavy toll of Japanese fighters and bombers.

Still hoping to achieve their goals through diplomatic pressure rather than all-out war, the Japanese government opened negotiations with the United States in March 1941. While Japanese Ambassador Nomura Kichisaburo outlined Japanese proposals—basically, a promise to behave in Southeast Asia if the United States would restore normal trade relations and abandon China—to U.S. Secretary of State Cordell Hull, the Japanese Foreign Minister, Matsuoka Yosuke, journeyed to Moscow where, in April 1941, he concluded a Neutrality Pact with the Soviet Union, thereby securing Japan's northern flank. "Now," said a jovial Stalin to Matsuoka, "Japan can move south." The Americans were far from pleased by this development—furthermore, Magic had revealed to them in considerable detail Japan's plan to move into Southeast Asia and her preparations for War. Cordell Hull, on June 21, informed Ambassador Nomura of the American position. Japan was to withdraw from the Tripartite Pact, from French Indochina, and—most unacceptable of all—from China itself. In return for this the United States would "favorably consider" the reopening of normal trade relations.

If Roosevelt felt he could afford to take a resolute stand against Japanese aggression it was not only because he sensed public support for that policy. It was also because American war industry and rearmament were now gaining momentum. Reinforcements, supplies, and several squadrons of B-17 Flying Fortress bombers were being dispatched to American forces in the Philippines. The American commander there, General Douglas MacArthur, was confident of his ability to fend off Japanese attack until the U.S. Pacific Fleet could fight its way to his relief. Indeed, Anglo-American plans for war in the Pacific had been concerted as early as 1938. The British fleet, based in Singapore, and the American fleet, based on Cavite in the Philippines, would blockade Japan while Anglo-American forces gathered to destroy her empire. Although Britain's resources were now fully committed to the struggle against Hitler, Winston Churchill, ever sensitive to the interests of his undeclared American ally, was prepared to dispatch sizable British military and naval reinforcements to the Far East.

Having made no progress in their American negotiations, the Japanese, in July 1941, forced the hapless French to accept their "protective occupation" of all of Indochina. This leap to the south posed a very clear strategic threat to both British Singapore and the Philippines. From Saigon Japanese ships and planes could dominate Southeast Asian waters. American reaction to this step was as swift as it was unexpected by the Konoye government—FDR immediately "froze" all Japanese financial assets in the United States and declared a total embargo on trade of any kind with Japan. England and the Dutch government-in-exile which still ruled Indonesia followed suit.

This hurt. Fully 67 percent of all Japanese imports came from the Anglo-American nations or their colonies. But of absolutely vital consequence was the fact that Japan imported more than 80 percent of its oil from the United States. Now this essential source was cut off at one blow—nor could Japan purchase oil from Indonesia in view of the Dutch embargo. Fuel supplies for the Imperial Navy would last two years at the most, only a year and a half in the event of war. The oil embargo created an immediate crisis among Japan's leaders; they had maneuvered their way into a corner. To secure oil they would have to either accept American terms, which, in view of the heavy sacrifices the Japanese people had borne to conquer China, might well provoke revolution, or conquer Indonesian oil, which meant all-out war against the West. Furthermore, they had to reach a decision swiftly—for if negotiations with the United States should prove fruitless, then Japan had to wage war while she still had sufficient reserves of oil to conquer more oil. Japan's military and naval commanders set the outside limit for a resolution to the problem as December 1941. If Japan did not fight before that time, she would lack the oil to do so later. The crisis provoked the downfall of the Konoye government in October 1941; the Prime Minister was replaced by General Tojo Hideki, a rabid militarist.

Two months before Tojo's accession to power, in August 1941, Roosevelt and Churchill had met at sea off the coast of Newfoundland. This "Atlantic Conference" took place during a low ebb in Allied fortunes: Hitler's Panzer armies were closing in on Moscow as Russian collapse seemed near, while his U-boats were raising havoc along the American North Atlantic lifeline to England. Initial English victories against Italian forces in North Africa were now jeopardized by the arrival of a German Afrika Korps—commanded by Hitler's "Desert Fox," Field Marshal Erwin Rommel—which had driven the British back into Egypt. Japanese intentions in Asia were clear. FDR, fearing he might be impeached if he went any further to help Britain on a practical level, was left with only words for weapons. He and Churchill issued an "Atlantic Charter" which, while no more than a noble description of the world they hoped would emerge from the war, by aligning the United States with Britain, might serve as a warning to Hitler and also provide a much-needed boost to British morale. Nonetheless, its issuance called forth a storm of abuse from appeasers, neutralists, and isolationists in the United States upon the President's head. Nothing, it seemed, could bring Americans to an awareness of their vital interests.

But the lesson was on its way. For during the summer and fall of 1941, the Japanese military and naval staffs in Tokyo completed their plans for all-out war. This would commence with a daring attack upon the U.S. Pacific Fleet at its base in Hawaii. Simultaneously, British and American bases in Malaya, Hong

Kong, and the Philippines would be neutralized by heavy air attack. With the Royal Navy and the American fleet unable to intervene, Japanese forces would quickly conquer all of Southeast Asia up to India and Australia, as well as the mid-Pacific American "stepping-stone" islands. This would create an impenetrable shield of Japanese military and naval force against which the Anglo-American forces might later dash themselves hopelessly to pieces. Tiring of bloody losses, in the long run Britain and the United States would accept Japanese domination of the entire Far East.

While Japanese leaders had little doubt of their ability to speedily carve out this vast new empire, some among them, especially the Naval High Command, were not at all sanguine about Japan's prospects of winning a prolonged struggle against the West. Therefore negotiations were to be continued in Washington until the last possible moment in hopes of arriving at a peaceful solution. The last possible moment would come when a Japanese Carrier Task Force was close enough to Hawaii to launch its planes against the American fleet at Pearl Harbor.

Epilogue

Day of Infamy

By midmorning on Sunday, December 7, 1941, Admiral Husband E. Kimmel, Commander in Chief of the U.S. Pacific Fleet, knew that his forces had suffered the worst defeat in American history. Reports pouring in from all over the islands, placed before him by white-faced, shaken aides, confirmed the extent of the disaster: the Army's Schofield Barracks and other installations wrecked and burning; the Air Corps' Hickam, Wheeler, and Bellows fields bombed into rubble; 188 American planes destroyed, most on the ground, and another 63 badly damaged; more than one thousand men dead, another two thousand wounded. Worst of all was the scene Kimmel could see for himself through the windows of his command post: thousands of tons of oily black smoke filling the sky above Pearl Harbor—the funeral pyre of the Pacific Fleet. There at their "protected" anchorage, four American battleships and seven smaller vessels had been sunk; four other battleships and three cruisers had been so severely damaged as to be rendered useless for months to come. The Admiral had lost an entire navy. And he knew who would be blamed.

The Japanese, it appeared, had launched their strike from six aircraft carriers which had somehow slipped through American patrols from the northwest. Within three hours 360 of their high-level, dive-and-torpedo bombers had completely altered the balance of power in the Pacific—at a loss of only 29 planes. There had been warnings. For weeks now, Washington had been cabling "alerts" of various degrees—but nothing to indicate that December 7 would be The Day. Like the authorities back in Washington, Kimmel had expected the Japanese to strike at Malaya, Hong Kong, and perhaps the Philippines—late British reports had described Japanese invasion fleets streaming south through the China Seas. But no one had ever credited those "pint-sized Asiatics" with the daring, skill, and efficiency to attack America's "impregnable" Hawaiian base five thousand miles from their home islands. Now, it seemed, the American people would pay the price for their racism. And now, too late, a few Naval Intelligence officers recalled how Japan had opened her war against Russia way back in 1905....

In Tokyo, beyond the International Date Line, it was already Monday, December 8, when reports of victory began trickling into the headquarters of Admiral Yamamoto Isoroku, Commander in Chief of the Imperial Navy. Jubilation among the younger staff officers was boundless. Japanese forces were landing almost unopposed in Malaya—they would drive south to take Singapore from the rear. Japanese planes had successfully bombed the American airfields in the Philippines, destroying MacArthur's air forces at a blow; now Japanese armies could land unopposed on the islands and quickly conquer them. Best of all, intercepted radio messages from Hawaii—the Japanese Task Force was steaming back to its home base under radio silence—indicated complete victory at Pearl Harbor. Nothing now stood between Japan and the conquest of the entire Southeast Asia area. Some of the bolder spirits among the naval staff officers were even wondering whether it might not be possible to conquer Australia and India. . . .

Admiral Yamamoto, although well pleased with progress made thus far, did not share in his subordinates' glee. True, the Japanese tide of conquest would now probably roll almost unopposed to its preset limits east of Burma and north of Australia—the Admiral regarded any further expansion as idiotic—and now Japan would be possessed of the oil, rubber, and other resources she required to maintain herself. But Yamamoto had traveled often and extensively in the United States in earlier days. He knew something of American industrial might. The fleet he had sunk today, the planes destroyed—all would be replaced with greater speed than his compatriots imagined. Nor was he so sure that American morale would collapse now, as had Russian morale after Admiral Togo's attack on Port Arthur. And what unkind fate had decreed that the American aircraft carriers (Yamamoto understood their importance if his enemies did not) should be absent from Pearl Harbor when the blow fell? Would the defensive ring that Japan was about to build, stretching from the Aleutian Islands through New Guinea to the Indian border, hold against the inevitable American counterattack? Yamamoto was not so confident about this as were others. But despite his worries, the Admiral could at least report initial victory to the Emperor....

Adolf Hitler received the news of Pearl Harbor at his command post, Wolfsschanze (wolf's lair), on the Russian front late in the afternoon of December 7. The Führer was elated. "We cannot lose the war!" he shouted. "Now we have a partner who has not been defeated in three thousand years!" Just a few days earlier, on November 28, he had tried to persuade the Japanese Ambassador, General Oshima Hiroshi, that Japan should go to war against the United States and Britain—but he had never expected so sudden, bold, and prompt a stroke.

Hitler's attitude toward the United States had hardened recently. With victory in sight in Russia, he had felt free to order his U-boat commanders to commence all-out operations against American shipping in the Atlantic. True, the beastly Russian winter and unexpectedly tough Russian resistance had prevented him from capturing Moscow—but there would be another German offensive in the spring and it would surely finish off the Soviets. It was time now to cut the American lifeline to Britain—and to teach the United States a lesson. He would hurry back to Berlin and there declare war against Roosevelt and his hateful set of Jewish advisors. The Americans would know what it was to fight a war on two fronts. The Führer had nothing to fear from that "racially mongrelized nation."

Some of his advisors, Hitler knew, were against declaring war on the Americans. Why take on another enemy? If Germany exercised restraint now, would not the Americans devote all their energies and resources to the Pacific War, thereby minimizing aid to Britain and Russia and assuring victory in Europe? Hitler brushed aside these objections. "If we don't stand on the side of Japan, the [Tripartite] pact is politically dead," he said. "But that is not the main reason. The chief reason is that the United States is already shooting at our ships. They have been a forceful factor in this war and through their actions have already created a situation of war." The Führer did not mention another reason for his determination, but it may have been decisive. Into the hands of German Intelligence had come a long report of Anglo-American military staff conferences. Called the Victory Program, it outlined Allied plans to strike at Germany first, no matter what happened in the Pacific. So the Anglo-Americans were preparing a surprise, were they? Now they would once again learn that the Führer always struck first; it was they who would be surprised. As Hitler ordered his special train prepared for the trip to Berlin, he chuckled grimly about the dismay his declaration of war would cause in Washington. . . .

The British Broadcasting Corporation's announcer was still delivering the first details of the Pearl Harbor attack when Winston Churchill turned to American Ambassador John G. Winant and exclaimed, "We shall declare war on Japan!" "Good God," Winant spluttered, "you can't declare war on a radio announcement!" But Churchill could not be restrained. For more than a year and a half he had been begging for American help—and receiving it. Now FDR should see that Britain was a loyal friend. He immediately dispatched a declaration of war to Tokyo and to the Japanese Ambassador in London, ending: "I have the honour to be, with high consideration, Sir, Your obedient servant, Winston S. Churchill." The Prime Minister commented, "When you have to kill a man it costs nothing to be polite."

But while Churchill rushed into the Pacific war, many of his advisors were worried. They too, like certain Germans, thought that now American forces would be deployed entirely in the Pacific. What if Hitler did not declare war in support of his Japanese ally? Could the American President persuade Congress to take on the European dictators while fighting Japan? It seemed unlikely. But Churchill knew something they did not. He, and a handful of Intelligence officers in London and Washington, knew that the British Secret Warfare Services had prepared a bogus document entitled the Victory Program, purporting to reveal Anglo-American staff plans to attack Hitler. This document, labeled Top Secret, had been "leaked" to an American isolationist senator, Burton K. Wheeler, one of FDR's bitterest foes and one of the bigwigs of the America First movement. Intelligence planners had been confident that Wheeler's patriotism would not surmount his hatred of Roosevelt—that he would make the "top secret" document public. This assessment proved correct. The Victory Program was published in the rabidly isolationist *Chicago Tribune,* German Intelligence forwarded it to Berlin, and if Churchill was any judge of Hitler's character, the Victory Program would certainly incite the Führer into the great mistake of declaring war first.

Before he retired for the night, Churchill confided to his diary: "So we had won after all!...I had studied the American Civil War....American blood flowed in my veins. . . . I thought of a remark . . . that the United States is like 'a gigantic boiler. Once the fire is lighted under it there is no limit to the power it can generate.' Being saturated and satiated with emotion and sensation, I went to bed and slept the sleep of the saved and thankful."

In Washington, on December 7, Roosevelt was working on his stamp collection in the White House when Secretary of the Navy Frank Knox telephoned the terrible news from Hawaii. The President had himself wheeled into the Oval Office. From there he called to inform Secretary of State Cordell Hull of the news, only to learn that the Secretary was even then receiving from Japanese Ambassador Nomura and Special Envoy Kurusu Saburo the decision of the Japanese government to "terminate negotiations." The mild-mannered Hull, in his youth a master of Tennessee mule-skinner's invective, loosed a stream of profane abuse upon the heads of his visitors they would never forget.

While alerts and mobilization orders streamed from the White House and reports of the total disaster at Pearl Harbor came in, FDR commenced the task of composing the speech he would make to Congress, which had been summoned into joint session, on Monday, asking for a declaration of war against Japan. Those who observed him during these hours were to recall that while excitement and, sometimes, panic erupted all around, Franklin D. Roosevelt remained calm. To those of his advisors who fretted that now the American people, in their wrath, would devote all their energies to the conquest of Japan, leaving Hitler victorious in Europe, FDR replied that he was sure the Nazis would relieve him of embarrassment by declaring war—he knew as his advisors did not all about the

Victory Program strategem and, more importantly, of the undeclared war he had been waging on the Atlantic which would almost certainly force Hitler's hand.

Furthermore he felt that the campaign he had waged to alert the people to the menace of Nazism had succeeded. Certainly the country was better prepared for the struggle than it had been a year earlier. True, the Selective Service Act and hence the new American Army had been renewed in the Senate a month ago by exactly one vote; but now that the United States had been attacked, he was confident that the forces of neutralism, appeasement, and the America First mentality would be smothered in an upsurge of patriotic fervor. The road ahead would be dark and grim, but he would lead the country through the nightmare of total war as he had led it through the nightmare of total depression.

On an autumn evening in Philadelphia long ago, FDR had warned "this generation of Americans" that they had "a rendezvous with destiny." The road between the wars that led to that rendezvous had been filled with shattered dreams, defeated hopes, mistakes, illusions, and bitterness. Now, at whatever terrible cost, a new way into the future would have to be found. The President, turning to the task at hand, began working on his speech. "Yesterday," he wrote, "December 7, 1941—a date which will live in infamy..."

Bibliography

Albrecht-Carrié, R. *Italy at the Paris Peace Conference*. New York, 1938.

——. *Italy from Napoleon to Mussolini*. New York, 1950.

Allen, William S. *The Nazi Seizure of Power*. Chicago, 1965.

Alvarez del Vayo, Julio. *Freedom's Battle*. New York, 1940.

Baker, Ray S. *Woodrow Wilson*. New York, 1939.

Balabanoff, Angelica. *My Life As a Rebel*. London, 1938.

Beasley, W. G. *The Meiji Restoration*. Stanford, 1972.

Benns, F. Lee, and Seldon, Mary E. *Europe, 1914–1939*. New York, 1965.

Bergamini, David. *Japan's Imperial Conspiracy*. Lexington, 1970.

Bishop, Joseph B. *Theodore Roosevelt and His Times*. New York, 1920.

Blackstock, Paul W. *The Secret Road to World War II*. Chicago, 1969.

Borkenau, Franz. *The Spanish Cockpit*. London, 1937.

Brenan, Gerald. *The Spanish Labyrinth*. New York, 1943.

Brook-Sheppard, Gordon. *The Anschluss*. New York, 1963.

Brown, Anthony C. *Bodyguard of Lies*. New York, 1975.

Bullock, Alan. *Hitler: A Study in Tyranny*. New York, 1961.

Butow, Robert J. C. *Tojo and the Coming of the War*. Stanford, 1961.

Byas, Hugh. *Government by Assassination*. New York, 1942.

Carr, Edward H. *The Bolshevik Revolution*. New York, 1953.

Carr, William. *A History of Germany*. New York, 1969.

Chabod, F. *A History of Italian Fascism*, tr. M. Grindrod. London, 1963.

Churchill, Winston S. *The Second World War*. Boston, 1949.

Clough, Shepard B. *The Economic History of Modern Italy*. New York, 1964.

Cole, G. D. H. *A History of Socialist Thought*. London, 1956.

Conroy, Hilary. *The Japanese Seizure of Korea*. Philadelphia, 1960.

Degras, Jane. *The Communist International, 1919–1943*. New York, 1956.

Dennett, Tyler. *Roosevelt and the Russo-Japanese War*. New York, 1925.

Eden, Anthony. *Facing the Dictators*. London, 1962.

————. *The Reckoning*. Boston, 1965.

Feiling, Keith. *The Life of Neville Chamberlain*. London, 1946.

Feis, Herbert. *Churchill-Roosevelt-Stalin*. Princeton, 1957.

————. *The Road to Pearl Harbor*. Princeton, 1950.

Fermi, Laura. *Mussolini*. Chicago, 1961.

Fischer, Louis. *Russia's Road From Peace to War*. New York, 1969.

————. *The Life of Lenin*. New York, 1964.

Garraty, John A. *Henry Cabot Lodge: A Biography*. New York, 1953.

George, David Lloyd. *The Truth About the Peace Treaties*. London, 1938.

————. *War Memoirs*. London, 1934.

Goerlitz, Walter. *The German General Staff*. New York, 1959.

Halperin, S. William. *Mussolini and Italian Fascism*. Princeton, 1964.

Hane, Mikiso. *Japan: A Historical Survey*. New York, 1972.

Herzog, Wilhelm. *From Dreyfus to Pétain*, tr. Walter Sorell. New York, 1947.

Hitler, Adolf. *Mein Kampf*. Boston, 1943.

Hough, Richard A. *The Fleet That Had to Die*. New York, 1958.

Hughes, Serge. *The Fall and Rise of Modern Italy.* New York, 1967.

Kennan, George F. *Russia Leaves the War.* Princeton, 1956.

——. *Russia and the West Under Lenin and Stalin.* Boston, 1960.

Kerensky, Alexander. *The Catastrophe.* New York, 1927.

Koestler, Arthur. *Spanish Testament.* New York, 1938.

Kohn, Hans, *The Mind of Germany.* New York, 1960.

Livingston, John (ed.). *Imperial Japan (1800–1945).* New York, 1973.

Lu, David. *From the Marco Polo Bridge to Pearl Harbor.* Washington, D.C., 1961.

Masur, Gerhard. *Prophets of Yesterday.* New York, 1961.

Matthews, Herbert. *Two Wars and More to Come.* New York, 1938.

May, Arthur J. *The Hapsburg Monarchy.* Cambridge, 1951.

Millis, Walter. *The Martial Spirit.* New York, 1931.

Monelli, P. *Mussolini: An Intimate Life.* London, 1953.

Mussolini, Benito. *My Autobiography,* tr. Richard W. Child. New York, 1928.

Nogueres, Henri. *Munich.* New York, 1965.

Nolte, Henri. *Three Faces of Fascism.* New York, 1966.

Nomad, Max. *Apostles of Revolution.* Boston, 1939.

——. *Rebels and Renegades.* New York, 1932.

Orwell, George. *Homage to Cataluna.* London, 1938.

Pares, Bernard. *The Fall of the Russian Monarchy.* New York, 1939.

——. *History of Russia.* New York, 1953.

Paxson, Frederic L. *Postwar Years: Normalcy*. Berkeley, 1948.

Reed, John. *Ten Days That Shook the World*. New York, 1919.

Rosenberg, Arthur. *The Birth of the German Republic*. New York, 1962.

Sansom, G. B. *The Western World and Japan*. New York, 1973.

Schlesinger, Jr., Arthur M. *The Age of Roosevelt,* 3 vols. Boston, 1957–1960.

Schuman, Frederick L. *Russia Since 1917*. New York, 1957.

Sheean, Vincent. *Not Peace But a Sword*. New York, 1939.

Shirer, William L. *Berlin Diary*. New York, 1941.

———. *The Rise and Fall of the Third Reich*. New York, 1960.

Smith, Dennis. *Italy: A Modern History*. Ann Arbor, 1969.

Stephenson, William. *A Man Called Intrepid*. New York, 1976.

Sullivan, Mark. *Our Times*. New York, 1926.

Thayer, J. A. *Italy and the Great War*. Madison, 1964.

Thomas, Hugh. *The Spanish Civil War*. New York, 1963.

Toland, John. *Adolf Hitler*. New York, 1976.

———. *The Rising Sun*. New York, 1970.

Trotsky, Leon. *History of the Russian Revolution,* tr. Max Eastman. Ann Arbor, 1961.

Tuchman, Barbara W. *The Guns of August*. New York, 1962.

———. *The Proud Tower*. New York, 1966.

Walworth, Arthur. *Black Ships Off Japan*. New York, 1946.

Warth, Robert D. *The Allies and the Russian Revolution*. Durham, 1954.

Wilson, Edmund. *To the Finland Station*. New York, 1940.

Wiskemann, E. *The Rome-Berlin Axis*. London, 1966.

Wolfe, Bertram D. *Three Who Made a Revolution*. New York, 1948.

Yoshihashi, Takehiko. *Conspiracy in Manchuria*. New Haven, 1963.

Zweig, Stefan. *World of Yesterday*. New York, 1943.

Suggested Reading

On the world before the Great War, read Barbara Tuchman's *The Proud Tower* and *The Guns of August* as well as Mark Sullivan's *Our Times*. Ray Stannard Baker's *Woodrow Wilson* is a standard biography; for the Paris Peace Conference also consult Lloyd George's *The Truth About the Peace Treaties* and Clemenceau's *Grandeur and Miseries of Victory*. Kerensky's *The Catastrophe* and Trotsky's *History of the Russian Revolution* are indispensable sources—Edmund Wilson's *To the Finland Station* provides a brilliant interpretation. George Kennan's *Russia and the West Under Lenin and Stalin* is definitive; on Mussolini and Hitler read

Laura Fermi's *Mussolini* and John Toland's *Adolf Hitler*. The United States during the Great Depression is covered in fascinating detail by Schlesinger's three-volume *The Age of Roosevelt*. Hugh Thomas's *The Spanish Civil War* has become the standard history of that conflict. On the era of appeasement, William L. Shirer's *Berlin Diary* and *The Rise and Fall of the Third Reich* give eyewitness views. On the Schwarze Kapelle read Goerlitz's *The German General Staff*. On FDR's secret war against the Axis consult Anthony Cave Brown's *Bodyguard of Lies* and Stephenson's *A Man Called Intrepid*. The first volume of Churchill's great history *The Second World War* describes the nightmare decade from a British viewpoint. About Japan, Toland's *The Rising Sun* is easy reading but Mikiso Hane's *Japan: A Historical Survey* is far more scholarly.

Index

ABOUT THE AUTHOR

Robert Goldston was born in New York City and attended Columbia University. A former Guggenheim Fellow, Mr. Goldston has written novels, documentary film scripts, and many works of popular history. An ardent traveler, he lived in England, France, and Spain after having "grown up all over the United States." Mr. Goldston now lives with his family in upstate New York.